AF616637

Seeing His Days

Jim Kay

Seeing His Days: A Treatise On The Seven One-Thousand Year Days of Redemption Based Upon The Complete Chronology Of The Old Testament by Jim Kay
Published by Creation House
A Charisma Media Company
600 Rinehart Road
Lake Mary, Florida 32746
www.charismamedia.com

This book or parts thereof may not be reproduced in any form, stored in a retrieval system, or transmitted in any form by any means—electronic, mechanical, photocopy, recording, or otherwise—without prior written permission of the publisher, except as provided by United States of America copyright law.

Unless otherwise noted, all Scripture quotations are from the King James Version of the Bible.

Scripture quotations marked AMP are from the Amplified Bible. Old Testament copyright © 1965, 1987 by the Zondervan Corporation. The Amplified New Testament copyright © 1954, 1958, 1987 by the Lockman Foundation. Used by permission.

Scripture quotations marked ESV are from the Holy Bible, English Standard Version, copyright © 2001 by Crossway Bibles, a division of Good News Publisher. Used by permission.

Scripture quotations marked EXB are from The Expanded Bible. Copyright © 2011 by Thomas Nelson, Inc. Used by permission. All rights reserved.

Scripture quotations marked GW are from God's Word® Translation, ©1995 by God's Word to the Nations. All rights reserved.

Scripture quotations marked NAS are from the New American Standard Bible–Updated Edition, Copyright © 1960, 1962, 1963, 1968, 1971, 1972, 1973, 1975, 1977, 1995 by The Lockman Foundation. Used by permission. (www.Lockman.org)

Scripture quotations marked NKJV are from the New King James Version of the Bible. Copyright © 1979, 1980, 1982 by Thomas Nelson, Inc., publishers. Used by permission.

Scripture quotations marked Phillips are from *The New Testament in Modern English*, Revised Edition. Copyright © 1958, 1960, 1972 by J.B. Phillips. Macmillan Publishing Co. Used by permission.

Scripture quotations marked RSV are from the Revised Standard Version of the Bible. Copyright © 1946, 1952, 1971 by the Division of Christian Education of the National Council of the Churches of Christ in the USA. Used by permission.

Greek and Hebrew definitions are from *Strong's Exhaustive Concordance.*

All charts, tables, and diagrams are created by the author unless otherwise noted.

Publisher's Note: The views expressed in this book are not necessarily the views held by the publisher.

Design Director: Justin Evans
Cover design by Judith McKittrick Wright

Cover: Arched pedestrian tunnel in the Jewish quarter of the old city of Jerusalem, Israel revealing light at the end of the tunnel. "But the path of the just is as the shining light, that shineth more and more unto the perfect day." Proverbs 4:18

Copyright © 2014 by Jim Kay
All rights reserved.

Library of Congress CataloginginPublication Data: 2014948483
International Standard Book Number: 978-1-62136-803-8
E-book International Standard Book Number: 978-1-62136-804-5

While the author has made every effort to provide accurate telephone numbers and Internet addresses at the time of publication, neither the publisher nor the author assumes any responsibility for errors or for changes that occur after publication.

First edition

14 15 16 17 18 — 987654321
Printed in the United States of America

CONTENTS

LIST OF CHARTS AND TABLES

FOREWORD

I have known Jim for almost fifty years. I was his pastor many years ago. He has always been a fervent Bible student, and he has constantly searched the Word to know what God has said and is saying. He not only searched the Word but he has lived the Word. When I read a book I want to know that the author lives what he is writing. Jim has lived his life for the Lord. I recommend this book to you.

—Leroy Cloud, Missionary to Thailand

PREFACE

I believed, therefore have I spoken.
—Psalm 116:10

During the year 1965 in Fremont, California, my pastor, Leroy Cloud, preached a message on Hosea 6:1–3 concerning "after two days…and the third day." There have been about two days (or about 2,000 years) since the first coming of Jesus and we are yet awaiting the "third day" (or 1,000 years) millennium. Seeking answers to truths contained in God's Word and with research during the years 1967–1970 at Bethany Bible College in Santa Cruz, California, I became interested in the Old Testament and what the Bible prophetically says concerning the end times.

Then, between the years 1980–1983, Bible teachers Kevin Conner, former dean of Portland Bible College, and Frank Damazio, now senior pastor at City Bible Church in Portland, Oregon, taught about the seven 1,000 years (days of the Lord). I purchased the book *God and His Bible* by W. H. Offiler during that time and studied it with accompanying chart of the seven 1,000 years. Also giving me great understanding was a textbook for a teaching entitled *Bible Treasures from the Book of Daniel and the Book of Revelation* by W. W. Patterson.

In December of 1998 I became increasingly interested in the study of Bible chronology to determine whether those things were true pertaining to seven 1,000 years. I wanted proof. I went to the Hal Bernard Dixon Jr. Pentecostal Research Center at Lee University in Cleveland, Tennessee. The librarian there had gathered up and laid aside some Bible chronology reference books for me to study when I arrived during the Christmas holidays.

After serious study of the recommended books and research on the Internet, I found that the most comprehensive and reliable work ever done on the subject of Bible chronology was *The Romance of Bible Chronology* by Martin Anstey. Another great Bible chronologist, Philip Mauro, condensed and refined Martin Anstey's work in *The Wonders of Bible Chronology.* In a phone conversation, Kevin J. Conner affirmed these two books to me when I told him of my interest in the subject. Kevin Conner's own book *The Seventy Weeks Prophecy: An Exposition of Daniel 9* has also proven to be an invaluable resource giving insights and understanding not found in most theological circles. Dick Iverson's book with Bill Scheidler, *Present Day Truths*, has given me further understanding of God's eternal plans and purposes during the past 2,000 years of church history.

I began to pore over the material and researched further. On several occasions I borrowed the book *The Romance of Bible Chronology* from Pasco County's intra-library program. *Nave's Study Bible* copyrighted in 1978 contains all of Anstey/Mauro chronological dates in the margins. There are very few of these original books extant today; however, I was able to purchase one from a Bible bookstore going out of business on the Internet. I now own both books.

Sir Isaac Newton once wrote:

> About the time of the end, a body of men will be raised up who will turn their attention to the Prophecies, and insist upon their literal interpretation, in the midst of much clamor and opposition…Amongst the Interpreters of the last age there is scarce one of note who hath not made some discovery worth knowing; and thence seem to gather that God is about opening these mysteries…The success of others put me upon considering it: and if I have done anything which may be useful to following writers, I have my design.[1]

Isaac Newton also remarked in a letter to his rival Robert Hooke, dated February 5, 1676: "If I have seen a little further it is by standing on the shoulders of Giants."[2]

In his essay, "Of Studies," Francis Bacon wrote: "Histories make men wise."[3] Bible chronologists who have studied Bible history and who have set forth an unbroken line of dates from Adam to Christ have contributed great wisdom into God's design of the ages.

I have prepared many tables and charts so that "they that know Him" may visually "see His days" (Job 24:1). While attending Portland Bible College, I received a chart in one of my classes with this quote from St. Augustine: "If thou shalt discern the ages, the Scriptures shall be open to you."

It is my prayer and desire to bring insights to God's people concerning God's design of the ages so that they might look with greater expectancy for that "blessed hope, and the glorious appearing of the great God and our Savior Jesus Christ" (Titus 2:13) and "*that, denying ungodliness and worldly lusts, we should live soberly, righteously, and godly, in this present world*" (v. 12, emphasis added).

Seeing His Days is a treatise on the seven one thousand year days of redemption based upon the complete chronology of the Old Testament.

> Why, seeing times are not hidden from the Almighty, do they that know him not see his days?
>
> —Job 24:1

> Moreover the light of the moon shall be as the light of the sun, and the light of the sun shall be sevenfold, as *the light of seven days*, in the day that the Lord *bindeth up the breach of his people*, and *healeth the stroke of their wound.*
>
> —Isaiah 30:26, emphasis added

> Come, and let us return unto the Lord: *for he hath torn, and he will heal us; he hath smitten, and he will bind us up. After two days will he revive us: in the third day he will raise us up, and we shall live in his sight.* Then shall we know, if we follow on to know the Lord: his going forth is prepared as the morning; and he shall come unto us as the rain, as the latter and former rain unto the earth.
>
> —Hosea 6:1–3, emphasis added

ACKNOWLEDGEMENTS

I WISH TO EXPRESS my appreciation to:

My God and my King, who has caused me to take up "the pen of a ready writer." He is my understanding, wisdom and inspiration as He imparts to me His infallible Word of Truth.

My wife, Ruth, who is my friend and a virtuous woman. In times of deep study she politely asks, "When are you coming up for air?" Ruth has been my supporter and encourager through the years and for that I am most thankful. She always stresses to me to believe God for greater things than I could imagine on my own. I love you, Ruth.

My children, Rhoda, John, and Anna, whom I love dearly and look forward to spending eternity with them and their families in the courts of our God.

There are many instructors in Christ, but not many fathers. I thank the Lord for men of God like Leroy Cloud, Dick Iverson, and David Garcia, who by their model and guidance have shaped my life into the very truths of the kingdom of God.

My friend, Armand Ternak, who has spent much time reviewing, correcting, and recommending changes to this book, for which I am most grateful.

To Creation House staff who through their work have guided and encouraged me all along in the formation of this book to be read by many.

INTRODUCTION

Why, seeing times are not hidden from the Almighty, do they that know him not see his days?
—**Job 24:1**

Known unto God are all his works from the beginning of the world.
—**Acts 15:18**

God that made the world and all things therein, seeing that he is Lord of heaven and earth,** dwelleth not in temples made with hands; **Neither is worshipped with men's hands, as though he needed any thing, seeing he giveth to all life, and breath, and all things; And hath made of one blood all nations of men for to dwell on all the face of the earth, and** hath determined the times before appointed, **and the bounds of their habitation; That they should seek the Lord, if haply they might feel after him, and find him, though he be not far from every one of us: For in him we live, and move, and have our being; as certain also of your own poets have said, For we are also his offspring.
—**Acts 17:24–28, emphasis added**

On Sunday morning, July 1, 2001, I was asked to pray for Israel. I prayed against the spirit of intifada (uprising) and resultant suicide bombings plaguing Israel. I also prayed that God would bless the people of Israel with salvation and ended with a partial quote from the following scripture:

> And there shall be upon every high mountain, and upon every high hill, rivers and streams of waters *in the day of the great slaughter, when the towers fall.* Moreover the light of the moon shall be as the light of the sun, and the light of the sun shall be sevenfold, as the light of seven days, *in the day that the* Lord *bindeth up the breach of his people, and healeth the stroke of their wound.*
>
> —Isaiah 30:25–26, emphasis added

After praying a portion of that scripture and with those particular words, I wondered what our pastor and his wife thought about what I prayed.

Seventy-two days later, on September 11, 2001 (9/11), terrorism brought down the Twin Towers of the World Trade Center in New York City and wrought great damaged to the Pentagon in Washington, DC. On that morning I was told that an airplane had crashed into one of the WTC towers. Later, when I heard that one of the towers had collapsed, I reflected on the Scripture passage concerning "when the towers fall." I asked a co-worker if *both* towers came down. He said only one tower, so I dismissed the thought, since Isaiah had indicated that it would be more than one tower falling. Moments later I learned that the second tower had fallen. It was then that I wondered if *this* was *that* spoken by the mouth of the prophet Isaiah. It was evident that acts of hatred and terror had been perpetrated against Israel and the United States of America. (However, there is the promise to God's people in the very next verse.) The "towers falling" and resultant tragedy left great loss of lives and a bleeding wound in the side of America's financial markets.

The word of Isaiah continued the theme by saying that "in the day of the great slaughter, *when the towers fall,*... the light of the moon shall be as the light of the sun, and the light of the sun shall be seven fold, as *the light of seven days, in the day that the* Lord *bindeth up the breach of his people, and healeth the stroke of their wound*" (Isa. 30:25–26, emphasis added).

The prophet Hosea gives the same type of imagery and wording:

> Come, and let us return unto the Lord: for he hath torn, and he will heal us; he hath smitten, and he will bind us up. After *two days* will he revive us: *in the third day* he will raise us up, and we shall live in his sight.
>
> —Hosea 6:1–2, emphasis added

A day with the Lord is as a thousand of our years (2 Pet. 3:8). It has been about two days (two thousand years) since the resurrection of the Lord. The third day speaks of the thousand year millennial reign of Christ when we will live and reign in His sight. Hosea exhorts us to follow on to know the Lord as we anticipate His coming as rain unto the earth.

> Then shall we know, if we follow on to know the Lord: his going forth is prepared as the morning; and he shall come unto us as the rain, as the latter and former rain unto the earth.
>
> —Hosea 6:3

God opened my understanding to Isaiah 30:25–26 about two years before the 9/11 tragedy when I was reading from Isaiah 30 in the foyer of our church and came to the place where he said, "The light of the sun shall be seven fold, as the light of seven days." My pastor, David Garcia, was just walking by and I began to exclaim to him about "the light of seven days" that had never been opened up to me in such a powerful way. I had been doing personal studies concerning the relationship of Bible chronology to the Scriptural concept that "one day is with the Lord as a thousand years, and a thousand years as a day" (2 Pet. 3:8).

This passage in Isaiah speaks of the *light of seven days*! It was March 2000 that I spoke at a men's retreat on the subject of "The Light of Seven Days" reflecting on 4,000 years of the Old Testament, the 2,000 years of the church age, and the 1,000 years of the millennial age yet to be fulfilled. We are living in the transition between the sixth and seventh one thousand year Days of the Lord.

As in other forms of life, God created and designed the human body with bilateral symmetry.

> Bilateral symmetry, or two-sidedness, in vertebrates, etc., is that in which the body can be divided into symmetrical halves by a vertical plane passing through the middle.[1]
>
> In nature and biology, symmetry is approximate. For example, plant leaves, while considered symmetric, will rarely match up exactly when folded in half.[2]

> Howbeit that was not first which is spiritual, but that which is natural; and *afterward* that which is spiritual.
>
> —1 Corinthians 15:46, emphasis added

The symmetry is never a mirror image on either side. There are subtle differences. And, likewise when comparing each 1,000-year period of Bible chronology, the beginnings of each 1,000-year era are not precisely 1,000 years, but close enough to say that it is "as" a thousand years.

Bringing this idea into perspective, notice the apparent divisions of the Old Testament chronology with transitional *key men* who were catalysts of change in God's progressive work in the redemption of mankind. Reckoning from the year of the creation of Adam onward, we find that the Bible contains a complete chronological design or pattern, not just vast amounts of chronological material. There is a continuous line of dated events which begin with the creation of Adam and which, unbroken, extend for forty centuries to the baptism, crucifixion, resurrection and ascension of our Lord Jesus Christ.

The word *chronology* is made up of two Greek words: *chronos*, meaning "time," and *logos*, meaning "a description." Breaking down the definition of *chronology* into phrases, we find:

- the science of ascertaining
- the true periods or years
- when past events took place
- and arranging them in their proper order
- according to their dates[3]

Merriam-Webster defines *chronology* this way:

- the order in which a series of events happened
- a record of the order in which a series of events happened
- a science that deals with measuring time and finding out when events happened[4]

From the creation of Adam to the manifestation of Messiah was a mere 4,000 years. In this span of time, God brought forth the Redeemer, the Lord Jesus Christ, and the New Covenant.

Martin Anstey explains it this way:

1. AN. HOM. = Anno Hominis = The year of the Era of Man, reckoning from the year of the Creation of Adam onward.
2. B.C. = The year of the Era before Christ, reckoning from the year B.C. 1 backward.
3. Bible Dates = The years of the dated events of the Old Testament according to the testimony of the Hebrew Text.

4. Ptolemaic Dates = The years of the dated events of past history, according to the "Received Chronology", based on Ptolemy's chronology.
5. The Ptolemaic Dates are about 80 years higher than the truth.
6. The Ptolemaic dates do not represent Bible chronological dates.
7. For the period between the Old and the New Testament Records they represent the Received Chronology adopted by Clinton and modern Chronologers generally.[5]

The first 1,000-year epoch begins with the first year of *Adam* in *AH 1* and extends to the birth of Noah in *AH 1056*, the Flood occurring in *AH 1656* when Noah was 600 years old.

The second 1,000-year epoch begins with *Noah* in *AH 1056* and extends to the birth of Abram in *AH 2008*.

The third 1,000-year epoch begins with *Abram* in *AH 2008* and extends to the beginning of the judgeship of Samuel in *AH 3003*. Samuel was the last judge of Israel and it was he who anointed both Saul and David as the first two kings of Israel.

Samuel was also a prophet. "Yea, and *all the prophets from Samuel* and those that follow after, as many as have spoken, have likewise foretold of these days" (Acts 3:24, emphasis added).

The fourth 1,000-year epoch begins with *Samuel* in *AH 3003* and extends to the birth of Christ in *AH 4041* (or *5 BC*). He was recognized as Messiah in *AH 4071* (or *AD 26*) and His Crucifixion was in *AH 4075* (or *AD 30*).

Observe that the commencement and transition from each 1,000-year period to the next is marked by *a major player* in bringing about God's *everlasting covenant* with man.

1. Adam = Adamic Covenant
2. Noah = Noahic Covenant
3. Abram = Abrahamic Covenant
4. Samuel = Davidic Covenant
5. Christ = New Covenant

Samuel's *judgeship* began in *AH 3003* and concluded in *AH 3023* at the anointing and kingship of Saul over the united kingdom Israel. However, Samuel was still ministering as prophet in *AH 3063* and anointed David king over Israel. God made a covenant with David (the Davidic Covenant) in Psalm 89.

> Why, seeing *times* are not hidden from the Almighty, do they that know him not *see his days*?
>
> —Job 24:1, emphasis added

Observe the 1,000-year divisions in the following charts:

The Seven 1,000 Years—Days of Redemption

"Why, seeing times are not hidden from the Almighty, do they that know him not see his days?" Job 24:1

Day 1

Adam	Seth	Enos	Cainan	Mahalaleel	Jared	Enoch	Methusaleh	Lamech	
	130	235	325	395	460	622	687	874	(Anno Hominis Dates)
+130	+105	+90	+70	+65	+162	+65	+187	+182	
4046	*3916*	*3811*	*3721*	*3651*	*3586*	*3424*	*3359*	*3172*	(Adjusted B.C. Dates)

Genesis Chapter 5

Day 2

Methuselah dies the year of the Flood –Shem was 98 the year of the Flood

THE FLOOD - 600th year of Noah's life = 1656 (2390)

Noah	Shem	Arphaxad	Salah	Eber	Peleg	Reu	Serug	Nahor	Terah
1056	1558	1658	1693	1723	1757	1787	1819	1849	1878
+502	+100	+35	+30	+34	+30	+32	+30	+29	+130
2990	*2488*	*2388*	*2353*	*2323*	*2289*	*2259*	*2227*	*2197*	*2168*

Genesis Chapter 11

Day 3

Abraham enters Caanan at age of 75-(2083) + 430 years until the Exodus (the giving of the Law = 2513)

Abrahamic Covenant — **Gal. 3:17 "The Law 430 years after" the Abrahamic Covenant**

Abraham	Isaac	Jacob	Joseph	*Joseph dies*	Moses	Exodus	*7 Years War +*	*Allot Land +*	*Period of Judges*
2008	2108	2168	2259	2369	2433	2513	2553-2560	2560-2573	2573-3023
+100	+60	+91	+110	+64	+80	+40	+7	+13	+450
2038	*1938*	*1878*	*1787*	*1677*	*1613*	*1533*			

Genesis 11 – 1Samuel 7

Day 4

Samuel (3003-3023)

"From the commandment to restore and build Jerusalem unto Messiah"

Beginning of Reigns Saul	David	Solomon	Solomon's Temple	Captivity Began	Captivity Ended
3023	3063	3103	3106	3520	3589
1023	*983*	*943*	*940*	*526*	*457*

Daniel 9:20-27

Decree of Cyrus in his 1st year & the return under Zerubbabel (3589)

(7 weeks=49 yrs.) + (62 weeks=434 yrs.) = 483 years 3637

The seven weeks (49 yrs.) = troublous times under Ezra & Nehemiah

1 Samuel 11:15 – Daniel 9:25-27

Ezra, Nehemiah, Haggai, Zechariah, Malachi

From 8th year of Saul's reign until Captivity = 490 years.

Jesus was baptized in water and became Messiah manifest in 26 A.D.

End of Captivity unto Messiah's Baptism (Anointing) = 483 years

457 years plus 26 years equals 483 years or 69 weeks.

Day 5

"We have found the Messias" John 1:41

Jerusalem was destroyed in 70 A.D. (Daniel 9:26)

Jesus Birth	Jesus Baptism	Crucifixion Resurrection	Apostolic Church	Persecuted Church	Imperial Church	Medieval Church
4041	4071	4075	4075-4145	4145-4358	4358-4521	4521-
5 B.C.	26 A.D.	30 A.D.	30-100	100-313	313-476	476-

The Gospels

(Reference A.D. Dates from "Present Day Truths" by Dick Iverson)

Day 6

Medieval Church (cont.)	Reformed Church	Modern Church	Pentecost Restored
-5498	5498-5693	5693-5946	5945-Present
-1453	1453-1648	1648-1900	1900-Present

Day 7

The Millennial Age

'Some of our able and painstaking chronolgers and expositors have adopted the mistaken estimates of **Ptolemy** as the foundation of their systems of dates, instead of grounding themselves upon the chronology of the Bible itself. Having committed themselves to a chronological scheme which makes **the era of the Persian Empire about 80 years too long...** and have accepted a defective chronology based upon heathen traditions."

Taken from "The Wonders of Bible Chronology" by Philip Mauro

Hosea's Prophecy Concerning Three Days

"Come, and let us return unto the Lord:
for HE HATH TORN AND HE WILL HEAL US,
HE HATH SMITTEN AND HE WILL BIND US UP.
AFTER TWO DAYS will he revive us:
IN THE THIRD DAY he will raise us up,
and we shall live IN HIS SIGHT.
Then shall we know if we follow on to know the Lord: his going forth is prepared as the morning; and he shall come unto us as THE RAIN, as THE LATTER and FORMER RAIN unto the earth. Hosea 6:1-3

Comparing Hosea 6:1-3 with Isaiah 30:25,26 and Psalm 90:4
And there shall be upon every high mountain, and upon every high hill, **RIVERS AND STREAMS OF WATERS** in the day of the great slaughter, when the towers fall. Moreover **THE LIGHT of the moon** shall be as **THE LIGHT OF THE SUN**, and **the light of the sun shall be sevenfold, AS THE LIGHT OF SEVEN DAYS IN THE DAY** that **THE LORD BINDETH UP THE BREACH OF HIS PEOPLE, and HEALETH THE STROKE OF THEIR WOUND. Isaiah 30:26**

For A THOUSAND YEARS IN THY SIGHT are but as yesterday when it is past, and as a watch in the night. Psalm 90:4

Ask ye of the Lord RAIN IN THE TIME of the LATTER RAIN:
so the Lord shall make bright clouds, and give them showers
of RAIN, to every one grass in the field. Zechariah 10:1

"Afterward shall the children of Israel return, and seek the Lord their God, and David their king; and shall fear the Lord and his goodness in the latter days." Hosea 3:5

The general purpose of this book is to challenge Christians, whether in church leadership or not, to become as the *Bereans* who "were more noble than those in Thessalonica, *in that they received the word with all readiness of mind, and searched the scriptures daily, whether those things were so*" (Acts 17:11, emphasis added). A more specific purpose is to help the reader *see* how God has fashioned and preserved the epochs of time from the first man Adam to the *last Adam*, who is the Lord Jesus Christ. Chronology from Adam to the close of the Babylonian captivity ends with the *Anno Hominis year of 3589.* The measuring of the 7 weeks (49 years) plus 62 weeks (434 years) for a total of *483* years of Daniel's 70 weeks prophecy (490 years) began *in the first year of Cyrus king of Persia* and extended to the baptism of the Lord Jesus Christ, *Anno Hominis year 4071* (date determined by inclusive reckoning[6]).

It was then that the Scripture says of Andrew, "He first findeth his own brother Simon, and saith unto him, We have found the Messias, which is, being interpreted, the Christ" (John 1:41). Then Jesus began preaching the gospel of the kingdom of God saying, "The time is fulfilled, and the kingdom of God is at hand: repent ye, and believe the gospel" (Mark 1:15). From Adam's creation to Noah's birth was *about* a thousand years (Noah was born Anno Hominis year *1056*). From Noah's birth until Abraham's birth was *about* a thousand years (Abram was born Anno Hominis year *2008*). From Abraham's birth unto Samuel's judgeship was *about* a thousand years (Samuel began his ministry Anno Hominis year *3003*). Samuel was a priest who anointed the first king of Israel (Saul) in Anno Hominis *3023*, was the last judge of Israel, and was a seer or prophet: "And all Israel from Dan even to Beersheba knew that Samuel was established to be a prophet of the LORD" (1 Sam. 3:20) From the beginning of Samuel's judgeship unto Messiah was *about* a thousand years.

Jesus, the Messiah who was called the Christ, was baptized in the river Jordan by John the Baptist in Anno Hominis *4071*. And so the forward movement of the epochs:

1. Adam to Noah (*1–1056*)
2. Noah to Abraham (*1056–2008*)
3. Abraham to Samuel (*2008–3003*)
4. Samuel to Christ (3003–4071)

Each epoch's duration was about a thousand years. The Old Testament witness? Psalm 90:4: "For a thousand years in thy sight are but *as* yesterday when it is past, and *as* a watch in the night" (emphasis added). The New Testament witness? Second Peter 3:8: "But, beloved, be not ignorant of this one thing, that one day is with the Lord *as* a thousand years, and a thousand years *as* one day" (emphasis added).

The expression "as" (Gr. *hos*) can be rendered "like"; in Psalm 90:4 the Hebrew "as yesterday," or *yowm*, may be rendered "day, time, or year, and yesterday" or "time past." God spoke to Jeremiah and said, "What seest thou...I will *hasten* [to keep watch of or to be wakeful over] my word to perform it" (Jer. 1:11–12, emphasis added). Throughout the ages God has been extremely careful concerning accounting for every consecutive epoch from Adam to the Lord Jesus Christ. The chronology set forth, compacted, and built together within the Holy Scriptures, cannot be broken up by heathen chronology. To base Bible doctrine upon a chronology that is not *in every way based upon Scripture* is contrary to the very redemptive purposes of God for mankind.

> epoch: A particular period of history, especially one considered remarkable or noteworthy or a notable event that marks the beginning of such a period. Medieval Latin *epocha*, measure of time, from Greek *epokhé*, a point in time.[7]

The apostle Peter warns believers:

But the heavens and the earth, which are now, by the same word are kept in store, reserved unto fire against the day of judgment and perdition of ungodly men. *But, beloved, be not ignorant of this one thing, that one day is with the Lord as a thousand years, and a thousand years as one day.* The Lord is not slack concerning his promise, as some men count slackness; but is longsuffering to us-ward, not willing that any should perish, but that all should come to repentance. But the day of the Lord will come as a thief in the night; in the which the heavens shall pass away with a great noise, and the elements shall melt with fervent heat, the earth also and the works that are therein shall be burned up. Seeing then that all these things shall be dissolved, what manner of persons ought ye to be in all holy conversation and godliness, Looking for and hasting unto the coming of the day of God, wherein the heavens being on fire shall be dissolved, and the elements shall melt with fervent heat? Nevertheless we, according to his promise, look for new heavens and a new earth, wherein dwelleth righteousness. Wherefore, beloved, seeing that ye look for such things, be diligent that ye may be found of him in peace, without spot and blameless. And account that the longsuffering of our Lord is salvation.

—2 Peter 3:7–15, emphasis added

Chapter 1
AVOIDING BIBLE CHRONOLOGY PITFALLS

He will deliver his soul from going into the pit, and his life shall see the light.
—Job 33:28

Conceptual Problems with the Starting Point

If a rocket to the moon is just three degrees off course when it leaves planet earth, by the time it reaches near the moon it will not hit its target but will be literally thousands of miles away from the moon. If we begin our theological concepts of Daniel 9:27 incorrectly, we will be very much off course by the time we get to our end-time charts.

> And he shall confirm the covenant with many for one week: and in the midst of the week he shall cause the sacrifice and the oblation to cease, and for the overspreading of abominations he shall make it desolate, even until the consummation, and that determined shall be poured upon the desolate.
> —Daniel 9:27

Frustrating and clouding the ability to visually "see His days" is the misinterpretation of the seventy weeks prophecy of Daniel 9. Many dispensationalists today start with the idea that Daniel 9:27 has to do with the Antichrist *making* a covenant with many for one week and then he causes it to cease or *breaks the covenant* in the middle of the week (the seventieth week). However, it is *Messiah* who *confirms* the covenant with many (His disciples). When Andrew told Simon Peter, "We have found Messias, which is...the Christ" (John 1:41) and where Jesus says in Mark 1:15, "The time is fulfilled," Daniel's prophecy of sixty-two weeks from the close of the Old Testament unto the beginning of Christ's earthly public ministry was fulfilled. From the time of His water baptism, Christ's crucifixion was three and one-half years (or one-half week) later.

This timeframe, from the commencement of Christ's ministry unto the Crucifixion, Resurrection, and His Ascension, represents *the first half of the seventieth week* (in other words, the sixty-nine and one-half weeks of Daniel's seventy weeks prophecy.) "And he shall confirm the covenant with many for one week: and in the midst of the week he shall cause the sacrifice and the oblation to cease" (Dan. 9:27).

The Last One-Half Week of Daniel's Seventy Weeks Prophecy

The last one-half week of the seventieth week is not prophesied to commence until the "little book" is opened spoken of in Revelation 10. "But thou, O Daniel, shut up the words, and seal the book, even to the time of the end: many shall run to and fro, and knowledge shall be increased" (Dan. 12:4) "And the voice which I heard from heaven spake unto me again, and said, Go and take the little book *which is open* in the hand of the angel which standeth upon the sea and upon the earth" (Rev. 10:8, emphasis added).

That which was shut up and sealed by Daniel *until the time of the end*, John was told to take and eat the *opened* "little book" (Rev. 10:9). After eating the "opened little book," John began to prophesy concerning the last half of Daniel's seventieth week. In Revelation 11 he speaks of the forty-two months in verse 2 and a thousand two hundred and sixty days in verse 3; in chapter 12 we find a thousand two hundred and sixty days in verse 6 and time, times, and half a time in verse 14; and in chapter 13 John tells of forty-two months in verse 5—all of which equal three and one-half years (the last one-half week) concluding the seventy weeks prophecy in Daniel 9. Only *three times* in the entire Bible does the expression "a time, times, and an half" occur: the prophecies in Daniel 7:25 and 12:7 and their prophetic fulfillment in Revelation 12:14.

> And he shall speak great words against the most High, and shall wear out the saints of the most High, and think to change times and laws: and they shall be given into his hand until *a time and times and the dividing of time.*
>
> —Daniel 7:25, emphasis added

> And I heard the man clothed in linen, which was upon the waters of the river, when he held up his right hand and his left hand unto heaven, and sware by him that liveth for ever that it shall be for *a time, times, and an half*; and when he shall have accomplished to scatter the power of the holy people, all these things shall be finished.
>
> —Daniel 12:7, emphasis added

> And to the woman were given two wings of a great eagle, that she might fly into the wilderness, into her place, where she is nourished for *a time, and times, and half a time*, from the face of the serpent.
>
> —Revelation 12:14, emphasis added

The "little horn" in Daniel 7:8 and 8:9 is *the same individual* as the dragon, the serpent, the Devil, and Satan in Revelation 12:9. This is the one who "wears out the saints" (Dan. 7:25) (in other words, persecutes the saints) and (as Daniel 12:7 says) "scatters the power of the holy people" (compare with Acts 8:1 how due to great persecution the saints were "scattered abroad"). The woman that fled to the wilderness and was given "two wings of a great eagle" (Rev. 12:14) to fly into the wilderness and be nourished (or supported) for a time, times, and an half is the last days church of the Lord Jesus Christ. The events of the last one-half week of Daniel's seventy weeks prophecy, prophesied by John in Revelation, extend from Revelation 11 through Revelation 19. The woman (the church) is preserved (not appointed to God's wrath)!

Pitfall of End-Time Doctrine Not Based Upon the Word of God

It is interesting that the book of Revelation records some fifty-seven sevens, but there are *no seven-year periods*. Too much of believed end-time doctrine today is *not based upon the Word of God*, but rather upon supposition and actually becomes what should be called "Christian fiction." Christian fiction then becomes accepted, glorified, and reverenced by believers even above the truth set forth in the Bible. The exalting of Christian fiction then becomes "Christian tradition," which is devoid of truth and is most difficult to break! The Holy Spirit is faithful and will reveal Bible truth to believers in these last days.

> John Darby divided the Bible into independent sections that either applied to Israel or to the church, no matter the result in dissecting the Word of God that way. The only natural outcome of this hermeneutical approach would leave scriptures addressed specifically to Christians such as the Gospel of John, the Book of Acts, the Pauline Epistles applied to the church and the rest of the Bible applied to Israel after the flesh…Darby's theology stated that the church of Christ has no part in God's covenant with Abraham, David or Israel. Darby saw the Christian church with the gospel of grace merely as an "interruption" of God's original plan with Israel. This interruption called "the church age" was unforeseen by Israel's prophets.[1]

George Müeller (1805–1898) once said:

> My brother, I am a constant reader of my Bible, and I soon found that what I was taught to believe did not always agree with what my Bible said. I came to see that I must either part company with John Darby, or my precious Bible, and I chose to cling to my Bible and part from Mr. Darby.[2]

George Müeller experienced a paradigm shift.

> A paradigm shift is when you view things one way and then you shift and view them another way. For example, at one time most all men held the paradigm that the earth was flat. Then, at a point in time, due to new information, men made a paradigm shift and began to believe that the earth was round. Paradigm shifts are in Scripture and they are part of your life and mine. Paul had a paradigm shift on the road to Damascus. He thought that Jesus Christ was a heretic and he was preaching against him. Then Paul met Jesus on that road and everything he believed about him was turned inside out. The person he preached against now became his life. That is a paradigm shift.[3]

Paradigm shifts may take a few days of revealed truth, as in the case of the apostle Paul on the road to Damascus, or possibly in some cases many years. "For precept must be upon precept, precept upon precept; line upon line, line upon line; here a little, and there a little" (Isa. 28:10).

The logic that the Antichrist is found at all in Daniel chapter 9 is fallacious because it does not stand the *hermeneutical test of correct grammar*. Edward Pusey, in his book *Daniel the Prophet*, says:

> He shall make firm a covenant with many during one week; and in the midst of the week He shall make sacrifice and oblation to cease. He speaks not of a temporary suspension of sacrifices, but of the entire abolition of all which had been offered hitherto, the sacrifice, with the shedding of blood, and the oblation, the un-bloody sacrifice which was its complement. These the Messiah was to make to cease three years and a half after that new covenant began, whether this was at first through the ministry of the Baptist or His own. It seems to be absolutely certain, that our Lord's ministry lasted for some period above three years.[4]

(Note: Edward Pusey is now allowed, by those whose extensive knowledge of Semitic literature renders them competent judges, to have been a sound and accurate Oriental scholar, and to have had an exact and idiomatic acquaintance with the usage of Hebrew words, even if they feel unable to accept his critical conclusions. The lectures on Daniel are acknowledged not only to be replete with learning, but also to sum up masterly the conservative position with respect to this part of the

Bible.) Pusey states, "And he shall confirm the covenant with the many for one week, (the prince had not been the subject of any former sentence; the covenant is, in Daniel, the covenant with God.)"[5]

"Of the prince" in Daniel 9:26 is a prepositional phrase of which the "prince" is the *object*. The *antecedent* of the pronoun "he" in verse 27 cannot be the "prince" since the word *prince* is the *object* of the prepositional phrase acting as an adjective describing the "people." Verse 26 has only two personal nouns that the "he" of verse 27 can reference, i.e., the "Messiah" and the "people." They are both *subjects* within that lengthy sentence. The "prince" is the *object* of the prepositional phrase describing "the people." The phrase acts as an adjective. *Nouns within the phrase cannot be the subject* of a sentence.

Jesus Christ Confirmed the Abrahamic Covenant

> Now I say that *Jesus Christ* was a minister of the circumcision for the truth of God, *to confirm the promises made unto the fathers.*
>
> —Romans 15:8, emphasis added

> *By faith he* [Abraham] *sojourned in the land of promise*, as in a strange country, dwelling in tabernacles *with Isaac and Jacob, the heirs with him of the same promise.*
>
> —Hebrews 11:9, emphasis added

In other words, Jesus Christ confirmed the covenant made with Abraham, Isaac, and Jacob (basically the Abrahamic Covenant). Jesus confirmed the Abrahamic Covenant during His life and ministry and ratified the *New Covenant* to His disciples the night before He was crucified. The New Covenant was contained within the Abrahamic Covenant:

> And as they did eat, Jesus took bread, and blessed, and brake it, and gave to them, and said, Take, eat: this is my body. And he took the cup, and when he had given thanks, he gave it to them: and they all drank of it. And he said unto them, *This is my blood of the new testament, which is shed for many.*
>
> —Mark 14:22–24, emphasis added

> Now to Abraham and his seed were the promises made. He saith not, And to seeds, as of many; but as of one, And to thy seed, which is Christ. And this I say, that *the covenant, that was confirmed before of God in Christ, the law, which was four hundred and thirty years after,* cannot disannul, that it should make the promise of none effect.
>
> —Galatians 3:16–17, emphasis added

> For *the law* having a shadow of good things to come, and not the very image of the things, can never with those sacrifices which they offered year by year continually make the comers thereunto perfect. For then would they not have *ceased to be offered*? because that the worshippers once purged should have had no more conscience of sins.
>
> —Hebrews 10:1–2, emphasis added

In the midst of Daniel's seventieth week, Christ (Messiah), by virtue of His perfect sacrifice at the Crucifixion, *caused the sacrifice and oblation to cease, to desist.* The veil of the temple was rent from top to bottom (Matt. 27:51). Jesus, God's only begotten Son, the only perfect and acceptable sacrifice, brought an end to the Mosaic ceremonial law; yet the moral law continues after the crucifixion of the Lord Jesus Christ.

> By the which will we are sanctified through the offering of the body of Jesus Christ *once for all.* And *every priest standeth daily ministering and offering oftentimes the same sacrifices, which can never take away sins*: But this man, after he had offered *one sacrifice for sins for ever,* sat down on the right hand of God; From henceforth expecting till his enemies be made his footstool.
>
> —Hebrews 10:10–13, emphasis added

The Necessity for Correct Grammar in Interpreting Scripture

In response to an inquiry made to the Jose Carillo English Forum about the grammar of Daniel 9 verses in question, Jose Carillo replied:

> By logic, all I can confidently ascertain is that the antecedent for the pronoun "he" in the line "And he shall confirm the covenant" is the noun "Messiah." . . . The noun "people," which is in the plural forum, obviously can't be the antecedent of the singular pronoun "he" in that passage, and this is regardless of whether "people" is the subject or just an object of a phrase . . . Now, regarding this question of yours, "Is there actually a rule in English grammar that says you must go back to the first noun to find the antecedent?", the answer is a categorical no. The proper basis for determining the antecedent is the sense and logic of the sentence or train of sentences in an exposition. No matter how many nouns may come between a pronoun and its antecedent, it is the evident meaning or the sense intended by the writer that prevails.[6]

The *antecedent* here must agree not only in *person, number,* and *gender, but also in case* (subjective or nominative case). To be correct grammatically, we cannot go back to a word which is in the *objective case* when the noun "he" in the phrase "he shall confirm the covenant" is in the *subjective case.* Bridging the grammatical gap in interpreting Scripture is the same for English or for Hebrew in this instance.

Case refers to the way a noun or pronoun is used in a sentence. When it is the subject of a verb, it is in the subjective case (the term *nominative* can also be used for subjective case though we will use subjective case only). Pronouns are used as subjects of verbs. *Subjective case of pronouns* should be used *when the pronoun is the subject of a verb.* Basically, a *pronoun takes the place of a noun.* A *subject pronoun must replace a subject noun.*

In Biblical Hebrew "a pronoun is a word that stands in place of ("pro") a noun. The word for which a pronoun stands (or refers back to) is called the antecedent of the pronoun."[7]

Further considerations of Daniel 9:27: There is a distinctive difference between two Hebrew nouns *zebach,* SC (Strong's Concordance) 02077 "covenant sacrifice," and *tamiyd,* SC 08548 "daily continual sacrifice." Also, translated "daily sacrifice" in Daniel 8:11, 12, 13; 11:31; 12:11, this word, *tamiyd,* is *only* mentioned throughout the whole Old Testament in the following passages:

> And to the office of Eleazar the son of Aaron the priest pertaineth the oil for the light, and the sweet incense, and the *daily* [continual or regular] *meat* [meal or grain] *offering,* and the anointing oil, and the oversight of all the tabernacle, and of all that therein is, in the sanctuary, and in the vessels thereof.
>
> —Numbers 4:16, emphasis added

> Beside the burnt offering of the month, and his meat offering, and the *daily* burnt offering, and his meat offering, and their drink offerings, according unto their manner, for a sweet savour, a sacrifice made by fire unto the LORD.
>
> —NUMBERS 29:6, EMPHASIS ADDED

> Yea, he magnified himself even to the prince of the host, and by him the *daily sacrifice* was *taken away* [SC 07311 *ruwm*, "to lift up, to take away"] and the place of his sanctuary was cast down.
>
> —DANIEL 8:11, EMPHASIS ADDED

> And an host was given him against the *daily sacrifice* by reason of transgression, and it cast down the truth to the ground; and it practised, and prospered.
>
> —DANIEL 8:12, EMPHASIS ADDED

> Then I heard one saint speaking, and another saint said unto that certain saint which spake, How long shall be the vision concerning the *daily sacrifice*, and the transgression of desolation, to give both the sanctuary and the host to be trodden under foot?
>
> —DANIEL 8:13, EMPHASIS ADDED

> And arms shall stand on his part, and they shall pollute the sanctuary of strength, and shall *take away* [SC 05493 *rwo*, "to be taken away, be removed"] the *daily sacrifice*, and they shall place the abomination that maketh desolate.
>
> —DANIEL 11:31, EMPHASIS ADDED

> And from the time that the *daily sacrifice* shall be *taken away* [SC 05493 *cuwr*, "to be taken away, be removed "], and the abomination that maketh desolate set up, there shall be a thousand two hundred and ninety days.
>
> —DANIEL 12:11, EMPHASIS ADDED

Also, compare and contrast Daniel 9:27 with the other references in Daniel (8:11, 12, 13; 11:31; and 12:11).

> And he shall confirm the covenant with many for one week: and in the midst of the week he shall cause the sacrifice [SC 02077 *zebach*, "covenant sacrifice"] and the oblation to cease (SC 07673 *shabath*, "to cease, desist, rest"] and for the overspreading of abominations he shall make it desolate, even until the consummation, and that determined shall be poured upon the desolate.
>
> —DANIEL 9:27, EMPHASIS ADDED

Notice that Daniel *does not* use the expression "take or taken away" in Daniel 9:27 as he did in Daniel 8:22, 11:31, and 12:11. Contrasting in context, "taken away" seems to imply a physical and perhaps violent "taking away" by a vile person, as in Daniel 12:11, while in Daniel 9:27 it says that "he shall cause the sacrifice and oblation to *cease*," that is, "to put to an end or to rest," just like God ceased from His work and rested on the seventh day.

The distinction between the two expressions "taken away" and "cause to cease" is shown below:

> And from the time that the *daily sacrifice* shall be *taken away* [SC 05493 *cuwr*, "to be taken away, be removed"].
>
> —DANIEL 12:11, EMPHASIS ADDED

> He shall cause the *sacrifice* [SC 02077 *zebach*, "the Passover, the annual sacrifice, the covenant sacrifice, sacrifices of righteousness:] and the oblation to *cease* [SC 07673 *shabath*, "to cease, desist, rest, put an end to"].
>
> —Daniel 9:27, emphasis added

> For the law having a shadow of good things to come, and not the very image of the things, *can never with those sacrifices which they offered year by year continually make the comers thereunto perfect.* For then would they not have *ceased* [SC 03973 *pauo*, "to cease or leave off"] to be offered? because that the worshippers once purged should have had no more conscience of sins.
>
> —Hebrews 10:1–2

Covenant of Death Not Related to Daniel 9:27

Some view the 'covenant' referred to by Daniel in chapter 9, verse 27, as being made by the Antichrist, but 'the covenant with death' from Isaiah 28:15, 18 actually is the 'covenant' or alliance that Israel makes with Egypt.[8] (See Isaiah 30:1–7 and 36:6–9.)

It is a *proposed league* with Egypt ("lies" and "falsehood") while professing loyalty to Assyria in the days of their dependence on Assyria into which Ahaz had brought them. An Egypt alliance (covenant with death) was to prevent any damage to themselves from an Assyrian invasion. Their expected help from Egypt will bring no rest or safety to them.

There is no evidence that Titus made any covenant with the Jews. Messiah is the main focus in Daniel 9, if we take the pronoun "He" as relating to *Messiah*, there is found in the New Testament scriptures a perfect fulfillment of the passage. The pronoun "He" grammatically must be taken as referring to Christ. There are virtually *no* scriptures of any prince, other than Messiah the Prince, *confirming a covenant* with Israel.

The Problem with Ptolemy's Canon (The Received Chronology)

> After much study of the entire subject, we are convinced that the Scriptures do not leave us in uncertainty as to those essential matters of fact. Indeed, it will be seen by what follows that, on the contrary, both events are marked and dated with unusual exactitude...Some of our able and painstaking chronologists and expositors have adopted the mistaken estimates of Ptolemy as the foundation of their systems of dates, instead of grounding themselves upon the chronology of the Bible itself. Having committed themselves to a chronological scheme which makes the era of the Persian Empire about 80 years too long, they have been compelled to construe the statements of Scripture in such wise as to force them into agreement with that scheme; and inasmuch as the measure of 483 years from the first year of Cyrus would, if Ptolemy's table be accepted, come short, by many years, of any event in the lifetime of Christ, one must either abandon that table, or else must search for a decree of a Persian King, many years nearer to Christ, to serve as the starting point of the Seventy Weeks of Daniel. The trouble, therefore, is not that there is any uncertainty in the Scriptures, but that expositors have turned aside from the Scriptures, and have accepted, for the 500 years immediately preceding the coming of Christ, a defective chronology based upon heathen traditions.[9]

The "Received Chronology," based upon Ptolemy's faulty canon that makes the reigns of the Persian kings about *80 years too long*, should become the "Rejected Chronology." And the "Adjusted Chronology" of Martin Anstey and Philip Mauro in their excellent works, *The Romance of Bible*

Chronology and *The Wonders of Bible Chronology*, should be called the "Accepted Chronology." Bible scholars, apostles, prophets, evangelists, pastors, teachers, theologians, and college and seminary professors, including their students, too long have tolerated the Received Chronology, which is not totally based upon Scripture alone. By accepting a chronology *based not entirely on Scripture* we will, without a doubt, err greatly in God's chronological scheme for the ages.

Chapter 2
MAJOR CHRONOLOGICAL LINKS

But the path of the just is as the shining light, that shineth more and more unto the perfect day.
—**Proverbs 4:18**

Martin Anstey defines *chronology* this way:

> Chronology is a branch of History. As such it is governed by the laws that determine the validity of the results reached by the process of scientific investigation and historical enquiry. It is also a branch of Applied Mathematics, and Mathematics is an exact Science. In a truly scientific Chronology there is no room for any date that is not demonstrably true. This view of the limits of the subject accounts for the absence of the note of interrogation (?) after any date in the chronological tables or charts set forth. Like Mathematics, Chronology has its axioms, its postulates, and its definitions, of which the most important and the most fundamental is the trustworthiness of the testimony of honest, capable, and contemporary witnesses, like that of the men whose testimony is preserved in the Records of the Old Testament.[1]

In my beginning studies in Bible chronology, I went to a vacant room in our church that had a table and chairs. I started in Genesis and methodically studied through the Old Testament, writing copious notes in my quest to search out the scriptures concerning these matters. I found that by using the Received Chronology there were just too many years using Ptolemaic dates. But after perusing the chronology books by Martin Anstey and Philip Mauro, I learned of the errors in Ptolemy's chronological scheme. By following *only* Bible dates, the baptism, crucifixion, resurrection, and ascension of our Lord *fit perfectly* with Daniel's seventy weeks prophecy as well as the AD 30 date for the Crucifixion. Below are two charts. The first chart shows eight major chronological Scripture links from Adam to the crucifixion of Jesus. The second chart shows the breakdown of Daniel's seventy weeks prophecy using *only* Bible dates coinciding with Martin Anstey and Philip Mauro.

The two charts below are a condensation of the author's personal study of Bible chronology:

Eight Major Chronological Scripture Links

Major Link	Anno Hom.	Adj. B.C./A.D.	Scripture
Adam to Noah	1 to 1056	B.C. 4046 to 2990	Gen. 5:3-32
Noah to Abrahamic Covenant	1056 to 2083	B.C. 2990 to 1963	Gen. 11:10-26
Abrahamic Covenant to The Law	2083 to 2513	B.C. 1963 to 1533	Gen. 11:32; 12:1; Acts 7:4; Ex. 12:40-41; Gal. 3:17
The Exodus to Solomon's Temple	2513 to 3106	B.C. 1533 to 939	Acts 13:20; 1 Kgs. 6:1
King Saul's 8th Year to Captivity	3030 to 3520	B.C. 1016 to 526	Lev. 26:33-34; II Chron. 36:20-21
Babylonian Captivity	3520 to 3589	B.C. 526 to 457	Jer. 25:11; Lev. 26:40-44; Dan. 9:2-3
Babylonian Captivity to Messiah	3589 to 4071	B.C. 457 to 26 A.D	Daniel 9:24-26
Messiah's Ministry to Crucifixion	4071 to 4075	26 A.D. to 30 A.D.	Daniel 9:27

Breakdown of Daniel's Seventy Weeks Prophecy

Period		Weeks	Years
Cyrus Decree and the Return (A.H. 3589-3637) (457 B.C.-409 B.C.)	=	**7 Weeks** or	49 Years
Inter-testament Period (A.H. 3637-A.H. 4071) (409 B.C.-26 A.D.)	=	**62 Weeks** or	434 Years
Baptism to Crucifixion (A.H. 4071-A.H. 4075) (26 A.D-30 A.D.)	=	**½ Week** or	3 ½ Years
Last ½ Week of Daniel's 70 Weeks Prophecy (Rev. 11, 12, 13)	=	**½ Week** or	3 ½ Years
(See Daniel 12:1-9 and Revelation 10:1-11)		**70 Weeks or**	**490 Years**

The events of Daniel 12:10–13 are *not* to be related to the last half of Daniel's seventy weeks prophecy, but are rather the prophesied events by Daniel in the time of Antiochus Epiphanes. These *last four verses* (12:10–13) are *not at all related* to Daniel 9:27 as Edward Pusey states of Daniel 9:27: "He speaks not of a temporary suspension of sacrifices, but of the entire abolition of all which had been offered hitherto, the sacrifice, with the shedding of blood, and the oblation, the un-bloody sacrifice which was its complement."[2] The last four verses rather belong to the "local prophecy" concerning Antiochus Epiphanes continued here from Daniel chapter 11.

Start of the parenthetical end-time vision given to Daniel

> And at that time shall Michael stand up, the great prince which standeth for the children of thy people: and there shall be *a time of trouble*, such as never was since there was a nation even to that same time: and *at that time thy people shall be delivered, every one that shall be found written in the book*. And many of them that sleep in the dust of the earth shall awake, some to everlasting life, and some to shame and everlasting contempt. And they that be wise shall shine as the brightness of the firmament; and they that turn many to righteousness as the stars for ever and ever. But thou, O Daniel, *shut up the words, and seal the book, even to the time of the end*: many shall run to and fro, and knowledge shall be increased. Then I Daniel looked, and, behold, there stood other two, the one on this side of the bank of the river, and the other on that side of the bank of the river. And one said to the man clothed in linen, which was upon the waters of the river, How long shall it be to the end of these wonders? And I heard the man clothed in linen, which was upon the waters of the river, when he held up his right hand and his left hand unto heaven, and sware by him that liveth for ever that it shall be for *a time, times, and an half*; and when he shall have accomplished to *scatter the power of the holy people*, all these things shall be finished. And I heard, but I understood not: then said I, O my

> Lord, what shall be the end of these things? And he said, Go thy way, Daniel: *for the words are closed up and sealed till the time of the end.*
>
> —Daniel 12:1–9, emphasis added

End of parenthetical end-time prophecy given to Daniel

Daniel's prophecy is resumed in Revelation 10 when John eats the *opened "little book"* and continues the prophecy in Revelation 11 (42 months and 1260 days), Revelation 12 (time, times, half a time), and Revelation 13 (42 months). (Read also: Daniel 7:25–26 with Revelation 12.)

Continuation of the local prophecy given to Daniel concerning Antiochus Epiphanes in Daniel chapter 11

> Many shall be purified, and made white, and tried; but the wicked shall do wickedly: and none of the wicked shall understand; but the wise shall understand. And from the time that the *daily sacrifice* shall be taken away, and the abomination that maketh desolate set up, there shall be a thousand two hundred and ninety days. Blessed is he that waiteth, and cometh to the thousand three hundred and five and thirty days. But go thou thy way till the end be: for thou shalt rest, and stand in thy lot at the end of the days.
>
> —Daniel 12:10–13, emphasis added

Albert Barnes has the following to say about the subject:

> Prof. Stuart, who supposes that the time is to be taken literally, and that the passage refers exclusively to Antiochus Epiphanes, explains the application of the language in the following manner: "Antiochus took away the daily sacrifice as is here declared. This was in the latter part of May, 168 B.C. Profane history does not indeed give us the day, but it designates the year and the season."[3]

It is the *daily sacrifice* (temporary suspension of sacrifices) being referred to here (i.e., *tamiyd*, "daily sacrifice," which was to be taken away (SC 05493 *cuwr*, "to be taken away, be removed") and not *zebach*, "the Passover, the annual sacrifice, the covenant sacrifice, sacrifices of righteousness." To the contrary, *zebach* was the entire abolition, sacrifice, shedding of blood, the oblation (the unbloody sacrifice which was its complement) as mentioned in Daniel 9:27 with the verb *to cease* (SC 07673 *shabath*, "to cease, desist, rest, put an end to").

> And from the time that the *daily sacrifice* shall be taken away, and the abomination that maketh desolate set up, there shall be a thousand two hundred and ninety days.
>
> —Daniel 12:11, emphasis added

Regarding Daniel 12:11, consider Keil and Delitzsch's statement: "In Daniel 12:11 the subject plainly is the taking away of the worship of Jehovah and the setting up of the worship of idols in its stead, for which the Maccabean times furnish an historical fulfilment."[4] (Please observe that there are two distinctly different nouns with two distinctly different verbs!)

The fabricated notion of building *another* future temple with ceremonies from the Mosaic covenant is incomprehensible in the light of these scriptures:

Behold, your house is left unto you desolate.

—Matthew 23:38

And Jesus went out, and departed from the temple: and his disciples came to him for to shew him the buildings of the temple. And Jesus said unto them, See ye not all these things? verily I say unto you, There shall not be left here one stone upon another, that shall not be thrown down.

—Matthew 24:1–2

But Christ as a son over his own house; *whose house are we, if we hold fast the confidence and the rejoicing of the hope firm unto the end.*

—Hebrews 3:6, emphasis added

God that made the world and all things therein, seeing that he is Lord of heaven and earth, *dwelleth not in temples made with hands*; Neither is worshipped with men's hands, as though he needed any thing, seeing he giveth to all life, and breath, and all things.

—Acts 17:24–25, emphasis added

Now therefore ye are no more strangers and foreigners, but fellowcitizens with the saints, and of the household of God; And are built upon the foundation of the apostles and prophets, Jesus Christ himself being the chief corner stone; *In whom all the building fitly framed together groweth unto an holy temple in the Lord*: In whom ye also are builded together for an habitation of God through the Spirit.

—Ephesians 2:19–22, emphasis added

Know ye not that *ye are the temple of God*, and that the Spirit of God dwelleth in you?

—1 Corinthians 3:16, emphasis added

And what agreement hath the temple of God with idols? *for ye are the temple of the living God*; as God hath said, I will dwell in them, and walk in them; and I will be their God, and they shall be my people.

—2 Corinthians 6:16, emphasis added

Thus says the Lord: "Heaven is my throne, and the earth is my footstool; *what is the house that you would build for me, and what is the place of my rest*? All these things my hand has made, and so all these things came to be, declares the Lord. *But this is the one to whom I will look: he who is humble and contrite in spirit and trembles at my word.* He who slaughters an ox is like one who kills a man; he who sacrifices a lamb, like one who breaks a dog's neck; he who presents a grain offering, like one who offers pig's blood; he who makes a memorial offering of frankincense, like one who blesses an idol. These have chosen their own ways, and their soul delights in their abominations.

—Isaiah 66:1–3, esv, emphasis added

An *abomination* is something hated or polluted, that which is disgusting, filthy, or detestable. To *desolate* is to devastate, ruin, or ravage or to cause horror, severe and total destruction by war, plagues, or natural destruction; something brought to *desolation* would be empty of inhabitants (a house, a city, or a kingdom) (Lev. 26:31–33), lonely, laid waste, spoiled, deserted, uninhabited, destroyed, depopulated, or abandoned. "O Jerusalem,...your house is left unto you *desolate* [empty and ready for total destruction]" (Matt. 23:37–38).

Before the Cross the earthly manifestation of the heavenly tabernacle (sanctuary) was *natural*. The series of tabernacles or temples before the Cross: tabernacle of Moses, tabernacle of David, temple of Solomon, the rebuilt temple after the Babylonian Captivity and Herod's Temple. After the Cross the earthly manifestation of the heavenly tabernacle (sanctuary) is *spiritual* (the church). *God's purpose was not to dwell in temples made with hands, but in men's hearts.*

> Our fathers had the *tabernacle of witness in the wilderness*, as he had appointed, speaking unto *Moses*, that he should make it according to the fashion that he had seen. Which also our fathers that came after brought in with Jesus [Joshua] into the possession of the Gentiles, whom God drave out before the face of our fathers, unto the days of *David*; Who found favour before God, and *desired to find a tabernacle for the God of Jacob*. But *Solomon* built him an house. *Howbeit the most High dwelleth not in temples made with hands*; as saith the prophet, Heaven is my throne, and earth is my footstool: *what house will ye build me*? saith the Lord: or *what is the place of my rest*? Hath not my hand made all these things?
>
> —Acts 7:44–50, emphasis added

Chapter 3
CREATION OF ALL THINGS

The Six Days of Creation

Ah Lord God! behold, thou hast made the heaven and the earth by thy great power and stretched out arm, and there is nothing too hard for thee.
—Jeremiah 32:17

According to A. M. Hodgkins:

> "In the beginning God created the heaven and the earth." In that simple statement we have the Bible declaration of the origin of the material universe; and it is one in which faith finds reasonable foundation. Interpretation of method may vary, but the essential truth abides. The theories of Science are continually changing and may clash with Scripture, the ascertained facts never do. In the same way our interpretations of the Bible may clash with Science because we may not interpret it aright, but the Divine record in Scripture will one day be seen to agree absolutely with the Divine record in nature.[1]

Through faith we understand that the worlds were framed by the word of God; so that *things which are seen were not made of things which do appear.*

—Hebrews 11:3, emphasis added

The creation of everything was accomplished in *six twenty-four hour days*:

> For *in six days the Lord made heaven and earth*, the sea, and all that in them is, and rested the seventh day: wherefore the Lord blessed the sabbath day, and hallowed it.
>
> —Exodus 20:11, emphasis added

> In the beginning God created the heaven and the earth. *And* [ו , Hebrew *waw*, "to wit, or now"[2]] the earth was without form, and void; and darkness was upon the face of the deep. And the Spirit of God moved upon the face of the waters. And God said, Let there be light: and there was light.
>
> —Genesis 1:1–3, emphasis added

> "Waw" is the name of the Hebrew letter which is used as a conjunction. It can mean "and", "but", "now", "then", and several other things depending upon the context and type of waw involved. It occurs at the beginning of Genesis 1:2 and is translated in the KJV, "And [waw] the earth was without form, and void."...The most straightforward reading of the text sees verse 1 of Genesis 1 as the principal subject-and-verb clause, with verse 2 containing three "circumstantial clauses." This is what [Hebrew grammarian] Gesenius terms a "waw explicativum" [also called waw copulative or waw disjunctive] or "explanatory waw", and compares it to the English "to wit." Such a waw disjunctive is easy to tell from the Hebrew, because it is formed by waw followed by a non-verb. It introduces a parenthetic statement,

that is, it's alerting the reader to put the following passage in brackets, as it were—a descriptive phrase about the previous noun. It does not indicate something following in a time sequence—this would have been indicated by a different Hebrew construction called the waw consecutive, where waw is followed by a verb [the waw consecutive is in fact used before the different days of creation (see Creation at the academy (Dr. Doug Kelly interview)]. Thus the Hebrew grammar shows that a better translation of Genesis 1:2 would be, "Now the earth..." and it could be paraphrased, "Now as far as the earth was concerned..." It is as if the author of Genesis (under God's direction), by the use of such a joining word, is going out of his way to stress that there is no break between the two verses.[2]

Therefore, as explained above, there is *no gap in time*, between Genesis 1:1 and Genesis 1:2. There was no catastrophic event or lapses of time occurring between these two verses. It was simply the initial state of God's creative acts prior to the Spirit of God moving upon the face of the waters and, then, God calling forth the creation of light.

Many people who have written on Genesis 1 have attempted to make a very significant distinction between two Hebrew words found there: *bara* (אָרָבּ), "to create," and *asah* (הָשָׂע), "to make or do." But this argument will not stand when we look carefully at the use of these words in Genesis 1 and in other biblical passages related to creation. Compare these two lists on the following chart by Terry Mortenson:[3]

Bara-Asah

***Bara*: to shape or create**			***Asah*: to do or make**		
Gen. 1:1		created the heavens and earth	*Gen. 2:4*		made heaven and earth
Gen. 1:21		created the sea creatures and birds	*Psa.* 104:24	*	made the sea, sea creatures and land animals
Gen. 1:27	*	created man (both Adam and Eve)	*Gen.* 6:6		made man
Gen. 2:3	*	created and made all His works	*Gen. 1:31*		*all* that He made
Gen. 2:4		created heavens and earth	*Gen. 2:4*	*	made heaven and earth
Gen. 5:1		created man (both Adam and Eve, cf. 5:2)	*Gen. 5:1*	*	made man (referring to both male and female)
Gen. 5:2		created male and female	*Gen. 5:1*		made man (referring to both male and female)
Ps. 89:47		created all the sons of men	*Is. 43:7*		made, created and formed man
Ps. 104:30		created sea creatures	*Gen. 3:21*		made the sea, sea creatures and land animals
Ps. 148:5	*	created heavens, heights, angels, hosts, sun, moon and stars	*Ps. 121:2*	*	made the heavens and the earth
Is. 40:26	*	created stars	*Gen. 1:16*	*	made the sun, moon, and stars
Is. 40:26		created trees, rivers	*Is. 41:20*	*	done this, made the trees and rivers

So, making a strong distinction between *bara* and *asah* in Genesis 1–2 is as unjustified as making a distinction between "create" and "make" in English. It is true that in Scripture only God is the subject of the verb *bara*; men make (*asah*) things, but only God creates (*bara*). But God also makes (*asah*) things. The verbs alone cannot tell us how God created and how long He took to create.[4]

The Big Bang Theory

To say that everything was created from a "quantum vacuum fluctuation," which brought forth "a singularity" the size of a dime with a "big bang" in the beginning and then stretching creation over 13.8 billion years, and to never give credit to the Creator God (Father, Son, and Holy Spirit) is vanity, foolishness, and sin. *It took God six twenty-four-hour days to create the heavens and earth* (not billions of years).

> Because that which may be known of God is manifest in them; for God hath shewed it unto them. For the invisible things of him from the creation of the world are clearly seen, being understood by the things that are made, even his eternal power and Godhead; so that they are without excuse: Because that, when they knew God, they glorified him not as God, neither were thankful; but became vain in their imaginations, and their foolish heart was darkened. Professing themselves to be wise, they became fools,
>
> —Romans 1:19–22

> Also, he has put eternity [*olam*] into man's heart, *yet so that he cannot find out what God has done from the beginning to the end.*
>
> —Ecclesiastes 3:11b, esv, emphasis added

> Through faith we understand that the worlds were framed by the word of God, so that *things which are seen were not made of things which do appear.*
>
> —Hebrews 11:3, emphasis added

> Even as there shall be false teachers among you, who privily [secretly or craftily] shall bring in damnable heresies, even *denying the Lord that bought them*, and bring upon themselves swift destruction.
>
> —2 Peter 2:1, emphasis added

A geologic age does not have an evening and a morning as the days in Genesis. In Genesis 2:2 it is declared that God rested on the seventh day; and if this day were an age, God would still be resting. As it is, God has affected the whole plan of salvation: "But Jesus answered them, My Father worketh hitherto, and I work" (John 5:17). When the Hebrew word for day (*yowm*) is accompanied by a *definite number* (first, second, etc.) as it is in Genesis 1, *it always means a twenty-four hour day.* The divisions of time in Genesis 1:14 (days, seasons, years) are used only in connection with twenty-four hour days and not geologic eras.

Miracles in the Bible

Three miracles in the Bible are enough to show the grandeur and glory and might of our God in His creative acts. "In the mouth of two or three witnesses shall every word be established" (2 Cor. 13:1b). (There are at least 120 miracles recorded throughout the entire Bible.)

1. Aaron's rod that budded

Basically, the almond tree begins to bud in the fall of the year; yet it is not until the next year in January that the bud grows sufficiently to bring forth blossoms. The next step is that the almond tree requires bee pollination and mild temperatures and minimal rain. Then after the petals drop and the trees leaf out, the small almond "fruit" appear in mid-August to late October. It takes a whole year for the almond tree to bear fruit (nuts).[5]

It is written in Numbers chapter 17 that God performed a *miracle* that produced ripe almonds *in one night* from Aaron's "dead" rod!

> The LORD said to Moses, "Speak to the people of Israel, and get from them rods, one for each fathers' house, from all their leaders according to their fathers' houses, twelve rods. Write each man's name upon his rod, and write Aaron's name upon the rod of Levi. For there shall be one rod for the head of each fathers' house. Then you shall deposit them in the tent of meeting before the testimony, where I meet with you. And the rod of the man whom I choose shall sprout; thus I will make to cease from me the murmurings of the people of Israel, which they murmur against you." Moses spoke to the people of Israel; and all their leaders gave him rods, one for each leader, according to their fathers' houses, twelve rods; and the rod of Aaron was among their rods. And Moses deposited the rods before the LORD in the tent of the testimony. And *on the morrow* Moses went into the tent of the testimony; and *behold, the rod of Aaron for the house of Levi had sprouted and put forth buds, and produced blossoms, and it bore ripe almonds*. Then Moses brought out all the rods from before the LORD to all the people of Israel; and they looked, and each man took his rod. And the LORD said to Moses, "*Put back the rod of Aaron before the testimony, to be kept as a sign for the rebels, that you may make an end of their murmurings against me, lest they die.*" Thus did Moses; as the LORD commanded him, so he did. And the people of Israel said to Moses, "Behold, we perish, we are undone, we are all undone. Every one who comes near, who comes near to the tabernacle of the LORD, shall die. Are we all to perish?
>
> —NUMBERS 17:1–13, RSV, EMPHASIS ADDED

If God can perform this miracle in *one night* that normally would take a *whole year* in the natural, don't you think that *the creation of all things* could have been done in *six days*? In nature it cannot be done, *but with God all things are possible* (Matt. 19:26)!

2. The feeding of the five thousand men

> And when he had taken *the five loaves and the two fishes*, he looked up to heaven, and blessed, and brake the loaves, and gave them to his disciples to set before them; and the two fishes *divided he among them all. And they did all eat, and were filled*. And *they took up twelve baskets full of the fragments, and of the fishes*. And they that did eat of the loaves were about *five thousand men*.
>
> —MARK 6:41–44, EMPHASIS ADDED

Matthew adds the fact that women and children were also present and they too were fed! "And they that had eaten were about five thousand men, beside women and children" (Matt. 14:21).

Where did the loaves and fishes come from? Who baked the loaves and who prepared the fishes? Only five loaves and two fishes were sent with the lad, but 5,000 men in addition to the women and children were fed to the full. Just how long does it take to bake enough loaves of bread to feed 5,000 men plus women and children? Who took the time to catch all the fish enough to satisfy the hunger of thousands of people? *How old were the fish*?

As the bread, which probably consisted of ingredients like flour, water, salt, and leaven, the Lord Jesus created all that was required for a mature cosmos in stages of *just six days*.

> In whom we have redemption through his blood, even the forgiveness of sins: Who is the image of the invisible God, the firstborn of every creature: For by him were all things created, that are in heaven, and that are in earth, visible and invisible, whether they be thrones, or dominions, or principalities, or powers: all things were created by him, and for him: And he is before all things, and by him all things consist.
>
> —COLOSSIANS 1:14–17

3. The miracle at the marriage of Cana

> This beginning of miracles did Jesus in Cana of Galilee, and manifested forth his glory; and his disciples believed on him.
>
> —JOHN 2:11

> And there were set there six waterpots of stone, after the manner of the purifying of the Jews, containing two or three firkins apiece. Jesus saith unto them, Fill the waterpots with water. And they filled them up to the brim. And he saith unto them, Draw out now, and bear unto the governor of the feast. And they bare it. When the ruler of the feast had tasted the water that was made wine, and knew not whence it was: (but the servants which drew the water knew;) the governor of the feast called the bridegroom, And saith unto him, Every man at the beginning doth set forth good wine; and when men have well drunk, then that which is worse: but thou hast kept the good wine until now.
>
> —JOHN 2:6–10

From whence came the grapes, who treaded out the new wine, and how long would it take to make enough wine for *six water pots* (almost *nine gallons each*)?

Jesus, Creator of all things, did it instantly!

> For in him dwelleth all the fulness of the Godhead bodily.
>
> —COLOSSIANS 2:9

> This beginning of miracles did Jesus in Cana of Galilee, and *manifested forth his glory*; and his disciples believed on him.
>
> —JOHN 2:11, EMPHASIS ADDED

Note concerning dates

When moving forward in time from the creation of Adam, we do not go back to vast ages in time for the creation of the cosmos; but as scripture says, on the sixth day God created Adam and Eve. The terms *Anno Mundi* (the year of the era of the world), reckoning from the year of the Creation onward and *Anno Hominis* (the year of the era of man), reckoning from the year of the creation of Adam onward are *synonymous* in Bible dating for this author. But for the sake of agreement with Martin Anstey and Philip Mauro, we will use the Anno Hominis dating as we move forward in time, beginning with the creation of Adam, Anno Hominis 1 (AH 1) as the first full year of Adam's life.

> And God saw everything that he had made, and, behold, it was very good. And the evening and the morning were the sixth day.
>
> —Genesis 1:31

> For *in six days* the Lord made heaven and earth, the sea, and all that in them is, and rested the seventh day: wherefore the Lord blessed the sabbath day, and hallowed it.
>
> —Exodus 20:11, emphasis added

> Before the mountains were brought forth, or ever thou hadst formed the earth and the world, even from everlasting to everlasting, thou art God.
>
> —Psalm 90:2

> Ye are my witnesses, saith the Lord, and my servant whom I have chosen: that ye may know and believe me, and understand that I am he: before me there was no God formed, neither shall there be after me.
>
> —Isaiah 43:10

Angels Created on the Second Day of Creation

The angels were created on the second day of Creation. Psalm 104, like Genesis chapter 1, is *chronological* and *inclusive*. Psalm 104 is also poetical. The psalmist clearly and forthrightly sets forth the purposes of each day of Creation.

> Bless the Lord, O my soul. O Lord my God, thou art very great; thou art clothed with honour and majesty. Who coverest thyself with light as with a garment: who stretchest out the heavens like a curtain: Who layeth the beams of his chambers in the waters: who maketh the clouds his chariot: who walketh upon the wings of the wind: *Who maketh his angels spirits; his ministers a flaming fire*: Who laid the foundations of the earth, that it should not be removed for ever. Thou coveredst it with the deep as with a garment: the waters stood above the mountains. At thy rebuke they fled; at the voice of thy thunder they hasted away. They go up by the mountains; they go down by the valleys unto the place which thou hast founded for them. Thou hast set a bound that they may not pass over; that they turn not again to cover the earth. He sendeth the springs into the valleys, which run among the hills. They give drink to every beast of the field: the wild asses quench their thirst. By them shall the fowls of the heaven have their habitation, which sing among the branches. He watereth the hills from his chambers: the earth is satisfied with the fruit of thy works. He causeth the grass to grow for the cattle, and herb for the service of man: that he may bring forth food out of the earth; And wine that maketh glad the heart of man, and oil to make his face to shine, and bread which strengtheneth man's heart. The trees of the Lord are full of sap; the cedars of Lebanon, which he hath planted; Where the birds make their nests: as for the stork, the fir trees are her house. The high hills are a refuge for the wild goats; and the rocks for the conies. He appointed the moon for seasons: the sun knoweth his going down. Thou makest darkness, and it is night: wherein all the beasts of the forest do creep forth. The young lions roar after their prey, and seek their meat from God. The sun ariseth, they gather themselves together, and lay them down in their dens. Man goeth forth unto his work and to his labour until the evening. O Lord, how manifold are thy works! in wisdom hast thou made them all: the earth is full of thy riches. So is this

> great and wide sea, wherein are things creeping innumerable, both small and great beasts. There go the ships: there is that leviathan, whom thou hast made to play therein. These wait all upon thee; that thou mayest give them their meat in due season. That thou givest them they gather: thou openest thine hand, they are filled with good. Thou hidest thy face, they are troubled: thou takest away their breath, they die, and return to their dust. Thou sendest forth thy spirit, they are created: and thou renewest the face of the earth. The glory of the LORD shall endure for ever: the LORD shall rejoice in his works. He looketh on the earth, and it trembleth: he toucheth the hills, and they smoke. I will sing unto the LORD as long as I live: I will sing praise to my God while I have my being. My meditation of him shall be sweet: I will be glad in the LORD. Let the sinners be consumed out of the earth, and let the wicked be no more. Bless thou the LORD, O my soul. Praise ye the LORD.
>
> —PSALM 104, EMPHASIS ADDED

Please observe that the *sons of God* (referring to *angels* in Job 38:7) were there in celebration and were witnesses of the third day, but not man:

> Where wast thou when I laid the foundations of the earth? declare, if thou hast understanding. Who hath laid the measures thereof, if thou knowest? or who hath stretched the line upon it? Whereupon are the foundations thereof fastened? or who laid the corner stone thereof; When the morning stars sang together, and *all the sons of God shouted for joy*?
>
> —JOB 38:4–7, EMPHASIS ADDED

A very wise pastor once said that when the Bible is dogmatic be dogmatic, when the Bible is vague, be vague. It is surprising that some theologians have to find some other *means outside of the Bible* to prove that "demons" were created *before* Genesis chapter 1. They cannot stand a "vacuum" of things that they do not understand. Where do they get this information? *The Bible never tells us about the creation or origin of demons.* Demons are spirit beings and real personalities who are Satan's servants and are numerous. In the Bible they are depicted symbolically as: fowls of the air, serpents and vipers, locusts, unclean frogs, unclean birds all made to torment mankind. However, *we do know* that the devil, Satan, and the angelic hosts that followed him *after iniquity was found* in him (the whole realm of evil) were expelled from God's holy heaven:

> And he [Jesus] said unto them, I beheld Satan as lightning fall from heaven.
>
> —LUKE 10:18

> God spared not the angels that sinned, but cast them down to hell, and delivered them into chains of darkness, to be reserved unto judgment.
>
> —2 PETER 2:4

> And the angels which kept not their first estate, but left their own habitation, he hath reserved in everlasting chains under darkness unto the judgment of the great day.
>
> —JUDE 1:6

The Bible is silent concerning many things. Who would have known in time past that there would have been pianos as instruments in church today? Who would have known that man would go to the moon and return safely? "What hath God wrought!" (Num. 23:23), were the words transmitted on May 24, 1844, to officially open the Baltimore-Washington telegraph line. In the past these and many other things were not known to us, but they were known to God.

> Known unto God are all his works from the beginning of the world.
>
> —Acts 15:18

> The secret things belong unto the Lord our God: but those things which are revealed belong unto us and to our children for ever, that we may do all the words of this law.
>
> —Deuteronomy 29:29

God did not tell us of His acts *before* the creation of all things. And He tells us of very little concerning eternity future. But the God of Truth does tell us enough to know that as believers we will be with Him eternally! That is sufficient. God's Word has been consistently true for believers for over 6,000 years now, and we expect with great anticipation that "His truth is marching on" into eternity.

> If in this life only we have hope in Christ, we are of all men most miserable.
>
> —1 Corinthians 15:19

The Bible clearly tells us *twice* in the New Testament that Adam was the "first man." Therefore, *mankind was not created in a previous age.*

> And so it is written, The *first man* Adam was made a living soul; the last Adam was made a quickening spirit.
>
> —1 Corinthians 15:45, emphasis added

> The *first man* is of the earth, earthy: the second man is the Lord from heaven.
>
> —1 Corinthians 15:47, emphasis added

> And the Lord God formed man of the dust of the ground, and breathed into his nostrils the breath of life; *and man became a living soul.*
>
> —Genesis 2:7, emphasis added

> For thus saith the Lord that created the heavens; God himself that formed the earth and made it; he hath established it, *he created it not in vain, he formed it to be inhabited*: I am the Lord; and there is none else.
>
> —Isaiah 45:18, emphasis added

The description that Jeremiah gives in the passage below uses imagery from Genesis chapter 1. But Jeremiah is declaring by prophecy Israel's desolation and has no reference to the days of Creation, but rather speaks in regards to Jeremiah's present day!

> Make ye mention to the nations; behold, publish against Jerusalem, that watchers come from a far country, and give out their voice against the cities of Judah. As keepers of a field, are they against her round about; because she hath been rebellious against me, saith the Lord. Thy way and thy doings have procured these things unto thee; this is thy wickedness, because it is bitter, because it reacheth

unto thine heart. My bowels, my bowels! I am pained at my very heart; my heart maketh a noise in me; I cannot hold my peace, because thou hast heard, O my soul, the sound of the trumpet, the alarm of war. Destruction upon destruction is cried; for the whole land is spoiled: suddenly are my tents spoiled, and my curtains in a moment. How long shall I see the standard, and hear the sound of the trumpet? For my people is foolish, they have not known me; they are sottish children, and they have none understanding: they are wise to do evil, but to do good they have no knowledge. *I beheld the earth, and, lo, it was without form, and void; and the heavens, and they had no light. I beheld the mountains, and, lo, they trembled, and all the hills moved lightly. I beheld, and, lo, there was no man, and all the birds of the heavens were fled. I beheld, and, lo, the fruitful place was a wilderness, and all the cities thereof were broken down at the presence of the* LORD, *and by his fierce anger.* For thus hath the LORD said, The whole land shall be desolate; yet will I not make a full end. For this shall the earth mourn, and the heavens above be black: because I have spoken it, I have purposed it, and will not repent, neither will I turn back from it. The whole city shall flee for the noise of the horsemen and bowmen; they shall go into thickets, and climb up upon the rocks: every city shall be forsaken, and not a man dwell therein. And when thou art spoiled, what wilt thou do? Though thou clothest thyself with crimson, though thou deckest thee with ornaments of gold, though thou rentest thy face with painting, in vain shalt thou make thyself fair; thy lovers will despise thee, they will seek thy life.

—JEREMIAH 4:16–30, EMPHASIS ADDED

Chapter 4
SEEING DAY 1

Adam to Noah (about 1,000 years)

Remove not the ancient landmark, which thy fathers have set.
—Proverbs 22:28

The fifth chapter of Genesis gives the complete list of the antediluvian patriarchs. The chart below by Martin Anstey gives an excellent visual.[1]

Antediluvian Patriarchs

1.	**Adam created.** "This is the book of the generations of Adam. In the day that God created man, in the likeness of God made he him;" Genesis 5:1
130.	Age of Adam at birth of Seth. "And Adam lived an hundred and thirty years, and begat a son in his own likeness, after his image; and called his name Seth:" Genesis 5:3
130.	**Seth born.**
105.	Add age of Seth at birth of Enos. "And Seth lived an hundred and five years, and begat Enos:" Genesis 5:6
235.	**Enos born.**
90.	Add age of Enos at birth of Cainan. "And Enos lived ninety years, and begat Cainan:" Genesis 5:9
325.	**Cainan born.**
70.	Add age of Cainan at birth of Mahalaleel. "And Cainan lived seventy years, and begat Mahalaleel:" Genesis 5:12
395.	**Mahalaleel born.**
65.	Add age of Mahalaleel at birth of Jared. "And Mahalaleel lived sixty and five years, and begat Jared:" Genesis 5:15
460.	**Jared born.**
162.	Add age of Jared at birth of Enoch. "And Jared lived an hundred sixty and two years, and he begat Enoch:" Genesis 5:18
622.	**Enoch born.**
65.	Add age of Enoch at birth of Methuselah. "And Enoch lived sixty and five years, and begat Methuselah:" Genesis 5:21
687.	**Methuselah born.**
187.	Add age of Methuselah at birth of Lamech. "And Methuselah lived an hundred eighty and seven years, and begat Lamech:" Genesis 5:25
874.	**Lamech born.**
182.	Add age of Lamech at birth of Noah. "And Lamech lived an hundred eighty and two years, and begat a son:" Genesis 5:28
1056.	**Noah born.**
600.	Add age of Noah at the Flood. "And Noah was six hundred years old when the flood of waters was upon the earth." Genesis 7:6
1656	**The Flood.**

Philip Mauro, in his book, *The Wonders of Bible Chronology*, sets forth a very comprehensive *overview* of Bible chronology:

> 1. Genesis chapter 1 is a complete chronology of six days, giving the order, day by day of the main events of how God prepared a habitation for man and including the creation of man, male and female.
>
> 2. The creation of man supplies the first era, and from it the extended chronology of the Bible starts.
>
> 3. Genesis 5 contains pure chronology—it is a perfect specimen of chronology in its definiteness and completeness from the beginning to the end.
>
> 4. Every statement connects in the most exact way with the preceding and furthermore a simple arithmetical check is provided so the accuracy of the entire tabulation is insured.
>
> 5. Genesis 5's table begins with the first year of Adam and extends to the 500th year of Noah. It covers the entire epoch from the creation of man to the Flood 1656 years.
>
> 6. Genesis 11 is a similar chronological table which takes the 100th year of Shem as its era (or starting point) and extends to the birth of Abram.
>
> 7. In subsequent chapters of Genesis is contained the chronology from Abraham to Joseph which the succeeding books of Moses extends to the Exodus, and the wandering of the Israelites in the Wilderness.
>
> 8. In the historical books (Joshua to 2 Chronicles) is found the chronology of the nation of Israel from its entrance into the land of Canaan to its captivity in Babylon.
>
> 9. Finally from the later historical books of Ezra and Nehemiah and the prophecy of the ninth chapter of Daniel we obtain a span of the years from the captivity to the manifestation of Jesus Christ to Israel through the witness of John the Baptist, whose coming was foretold in the last book of the Old Testament.
>
> 10. The Old Testament scriptures contain a complete count of the years from Adam to Christ.
>
> 11. The entire course of the 4,000-year period compassed by Bible Chronology does not lie in plain view upon the surface of the Sacred Text. At several points it disappears beneath the surface so that seemingly there are several breaks in the continuity of the chronological record. For example the Scripture does not state the age of Noah at the birth of Shem (Gen. 5:32) nor that of Terah at the birth of Abram (Gen. 11:26), but in the case of each the seeming breaks the needed information is supplied by other scriptures, though in some cases it has been found only after diligent search and careful deductions.
>
> 12. It will be a matter of deep interest to trace out these half-concealed links between the several epochs of Bible History.
>
> 13. So as to chronological data, likewise in other categories of truth in doctrine some things of value are not found upon the surface, but must be diligently sought through the substrata of the Divine Word.[2]

The line of Cain should not be confused with the line of Seth! Some names are the same or similar in each line. Just remember that *there is no chronology* for the descendants of Cain. However, *there is chronology* for the godly line of Seth.

Descendants of Cain and Seth

Descendants of Cain	**Descendents of Seth**
(*no chronology*)	(*with chronology*)
Genesis 4	Genesis 5
Enoch	Enos
Icad	Cainan
Mehujael	Mahalaleel
Methusael	Jared
Lamech	Enoch
Jabel	Methuselah
Jubal	Lamech
Tubal-cain	Noah

The Days of Enoch

> And all the days of Enoch were three hundred sixty and five years: And Enoch walked with God: and he was not; for God took him.
>
> —Genesis 5:23–24

> And Enoch also, the seventh from Adam, prophesied of these, saying, Behold, the Lord cometh with ten thousands of his saints, To execute judgment upon all, and to convince all that are ungodly among them of all their ungodly deeds which they have ungodly committed, and of all their hard speeches which ungodly sinners have spoken against him.
>
> —Jude 1:14–15

Of all the descendants of the godly line of Seth, Enoch pleased God. He lived 365 years and without dying God took him from earth to heaven. Enoch's name means "dedicated." Enoch begat Methuselah, whose name in Hebrew means "man with a dart or sword" or in Greek "when he dies, it shall be sent."

> By faith Enoch was translated that he should not see death; and was not found, because God had translated him: for before his translation he had this testimony, that he pleased God.
>
> —Hebrews 11:5

Enoch was a prophet declaring God's righteous judgment upon all the ungodly.

Sons of God: Angelic or Human?

> And it came to pass, when men began to multiply on the face of the earth, and daughters were born unto them, That *the sons of God saw the daughters of men* that they were fair; and they took them wives of all which they chose. And the Lord said, My spirit shall not always strive with man, for that he also is flesh: yet his days shall be an hundred and twenty years. There were giants in the earth in those days; and also after that, when the sons of God came in unto the daughters of men, and they bare children to them, the same became mighty men which were of old, men of renown. And God saw that the wickedness of man was great in the earth, and that every imagination of the thoughts of his heart was only evil continually.
>
> —Genesis 6:1–5, emphasis added

Jesus said: "For in the resurrection they neither marry, nor are given in marriage, *but are as the angels of God in heaven*" (Matt. 22:30, emphasis added). However, some theologians today take Genesis chapter 6 to mean that some angels married women on earth. This is unacceptable teaching. "Are they not all ministering spirits, sent forth to minister for them who shall be heirs of salvation?" (Heb. 1:14). Angels *do not* have the capability to procreate. The Bible never says that fallen angels cohabited on earth with women. How foolish a notion!

Some men from the godly line of Seth in chapter 5 saw that the ungodly daughters of the line of Cain in chapter 4 were fair to look upon, they took them wives of all they chose; and from that union came forth great wickedness. And this unholy relationship brought about abnormalities. Just recall Nehemiah's rage regarding mixed marriages:

> In those days also saw I Jews that had married wives of Ashdod, of Ammon, and of Moab: And their children spake half in the speech of Ashdod, and could not speak in the Jews' language, but according to the language of each people. And I contended with them, and cursed them, and smote certain of them, and plucked off their hair, and made them swear by God, saying, *Ye shall not give your daughters unto their sons, nor take their daughters unto your sons, or for yourselves. Did not Solomon king of Israel sin* by these things? yet among many nations was there no king like him, who was beloved of his God, and God made him king over all Israel: nevertheless *even him did outlandish women cause to sin.*
>
> —NEHEMIAH 13:23–26, EMPHASIS ADDED

Also, consider the New Testament admonition:

> Be ye not unequally yoked together with unbelievers: for what fellowship hath righteousness with unrighteousness? and what communion hath light with darkness? And what concord hath Christ with Belial? or what part hath he that believeth with an infidel? And what agreement hath the temple of God with idols? for ye are the temple of the living God; as God hath said, I will dwell in them, and walk in them; and I will be their God, and they shall be my people. Wherefore come out from among them, and be ye separate, saith the Lord, and touch not the unclean thing; and I will receive you, And will be a Father unto you, and ye shall be my sons and daughters, saith the Lord Almighty.
>
> —2 CORINTHIANS 6:14–18

In God's Word the expression "sons of God" not only refers to angels but also those who "received" the Lord.

> But as many as received him, to them gave he power to become *the sons of God*, even to them that believe on his name: Which were born, not of blood, nor of the will of the flesh, nor of the will of man, but of God.
>
> —JOHN 1:12–13, EMPHASIS ADDED

The words *angel* or *angels* occur fifteen times in Genesis. If angels were meant for the "sons of God" in Genesis, the writer would, without a doubt, have used the term "angels" and not used the term "sons of God." The context concerns the godly seed of Seth in Genesis chapter 5. Old Testament references to "sons of God" referring to angels in Job 1:6; 2:1; and 38:7 make no difference. Context, context, context! The Bible does not contradict itself. Angels do not marry! *The Bible never said that the angels who left their first habitation were somehow changed to be able to procreate.*

The chronology of the Bible begins in Genesis chapter 5 and covers the entire epoch from Adam to the Flood (AH 1–AH 1656). Then Genesis chapter 11 begins the chronological scheme from the hundredth year of Shem unto the birth of Abram (AH 1658–AH 2008). Genesis chapter 12 continues from Abram and concludes with the events in the life of Joseph (AH 2259–AH 2369) in Genesis chapter 50 as shown in table below:

Chronological Table from Adam to Joseph

Patriarch	Year Born A.H.	Age at Son's Birth	Years Added	Total Life Span	Year Died A.H.
Adam	1	130	800	930	930
Seth	130	105	807	912	1042
Enos	235	90	815	905	1140
Cainan	325	70	840	910	1235
Mahalaleel	395	65	830	895	1290
Jared	460	162	800	962	1422
Enoch	622	65	300	365	987 trans.
Methusaleh	687	187	782	969	1656
Lamech	874	182	595	777	1651
Noah	1056	502	448	950	2006
Shem	1558	100	500	600	2158
Arphaxad	1658	35	403	438	2096
Salah	1693	30	403	433	2126
Eber	1723	34	430	464	2187
Peleg	1757	30	209	239	1996
Reu	1787	32	207	239	2026
Serug	1819	30	200	230	2049
Nahor	1849	29	119	148	1997
Terah	1878	130	75	205	2083
Abram	2008	100	75	175	2183
Isaac	2108	40	140	180	2288
Jacob	2168	91	56	147	2315
Joseph	2259			110	2369

Explanatory Notes: A.H. = ANNO HOMINIS = The Year of the Era of Man, reckoning from the year of Creation of Adam onward.

Chapter 5
SEEING DAY 2

NOAH TO ABRAM (ABOUT 1,000 YEARS)

And spared not the old world, but saved Noah the eighth person, a preacher of righteousness, bringing in the flood upon the world of the ungodly.
—2 PETER 2:5

THE FOLLOWING TABLE by Martin Anstey shows the lineage and dates from Noah to Arphaxad.[1]

THE NOAH-SHEM CONNECTION
(MARTIN ANSTEY)

[Anno Hominis dates appear below in ***bold print.]***

1056.	**Noah born.**	
600.	Add age of Noah at the Flood (Gen. 7:6).	
1656.	**Date of the Flood.**	
2.	Add years after the Flood when Shem begat Arphaxad	(Gen 11:10).
1658.	**Arphaxad born.**	

In his book The Romance of Bible Chronology, Martin Anstey says,

> The Biblical year is the luni-solar year. Time is measured by the revolutions of the sun. The feasts are regulated by the revolutions of the moon, and the relations within the solar year are adjusted, not by the astronomical calculation, but by observation of the state of the crops, and the appearances of the moon. The resulting system was perfect and self-adjusting. It required neither periodic correction nor intercalation.[2]

In explanation of John Kennedy's writings, Anstey continues:

> John Kennedy's [(fl.1752) Rector of Bradley in Derbyshire] exposition of the story of the flood shows that Noah was exactly 365 days in the ark, and explains Moses' method of computing in terms of the months of the lunar year [see Diagram on the next page for the year of the Flood], whilst measuring time in terms of the solar year...Kennedy's view of the infallibility of the Hebrew Masoretic Text, coupled with his feeling of certainty with regard to the results obtained from his mathematically exact astronomical calculations, accounts for the dogmatic tone which characterizes his works. This note of infallibility is very annoying to modern scholars, who rejoice in the larger liberty afforded by the method of hypothesis and conjecture!
>
> From the 17th day of the 2nd month of one lunar year to the 27th day of the 2nd month of the following lunar year is a period of 354 + 11 = 365 days; meaning, one complete lunar year and eleven additional days. These days will invariably consist either of parts of two distinct lunar years or else of

one complete lunar year and part of another. When the last day of the lunar year is also the last day of the concurrent solar year we have what is called a year of commensuration. Such a year was the year AN. HOM. 1655, the 599th year of Noah's life the year before the Flood.[3]

The following chart by John Kennedy is included in Anstey's book.[4]

Diagram of the Flood Year

According to

John Kennedy's *New Method of Scripture Chronology*

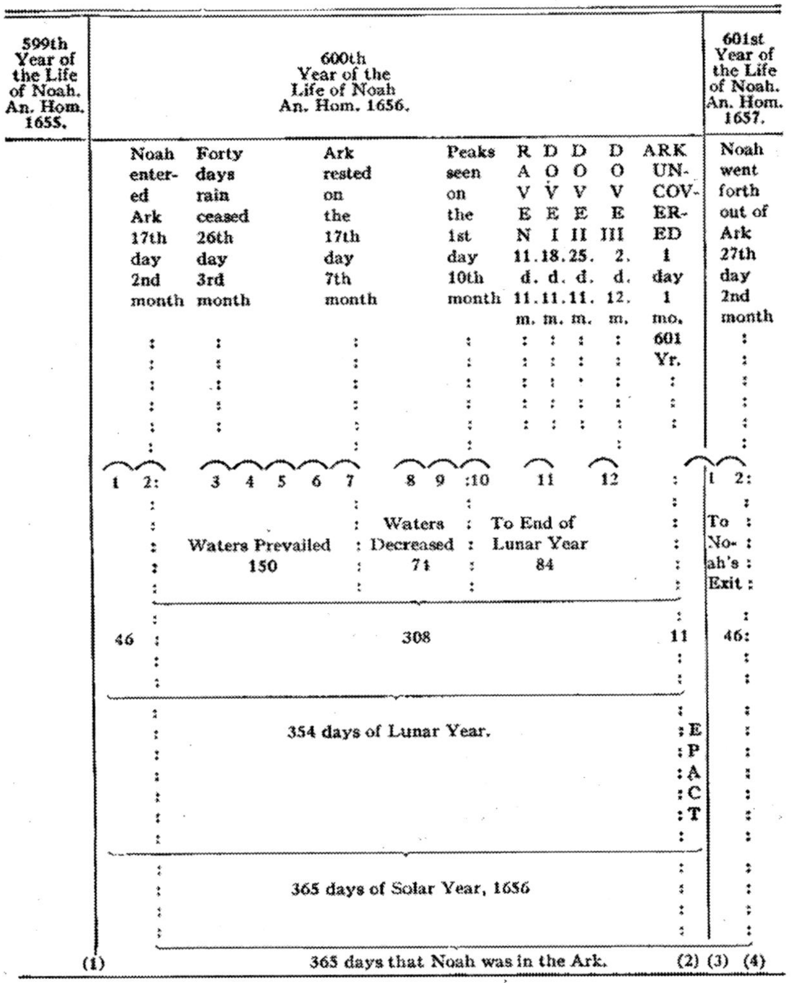

599th Year of the Life of Noah. An. Hom. 1655.	600th Year of the Life of Noah An. Hom. 1656.	601st Year of the Life of Noah. An. Hom. 1657.

Noah entered Ark 17th day 2nd month	Forty days rain ceased 26th day 3rd month	Ark rested on the 17th day 7th month	Peaks seen on the 1st day 10th month	RAVEN 11. d. 11. m.	DOVE I 18. d. 11. m.	DOVE II 25. d. 11. m.	DOVE III 2. d. 12. m.	ARK UNCOVERED 1 day 1 mo. 601 Yr.	Noah went forth out of Ark 27th day 2nd month

Months: 1 2: 3 4 5 6 7 8 9 :10 11 12 : 1 2:

Waters Prevailed 150 : Waters Decreased 71 : To End of Lunar Year 84 : To Noah's Exit

46 : 308 : 11 : 46:

354 days of Lunar Year. : EPACT

365 days of Solar Year, 1656

(1) 365 days that Noah was in the Ark. (2) (3) (4)

(1) Beginning of the Solar Year An. Hom. 1656, which this year coincides with the Lunar Year.
(2) End of the Lunar Year of 354 days.
(3) End of the Solar Year of 365 days.
(4) End of the 365 days that Noah was in the Ark.

Anstey continues:

> When the 1st day of the lunar year is also the 1st day of the concurrent solar year, we have what is called a year of coincidence. Such a year was the year AN. HOM. 1656, the 600th year of Noah's life. The Flood year occupied 319 days of the solar year 1656, and 46 days of the solar year 1657, the year after the Flood. It also occupied 308 days of the lunar year concurrent with the solar year 1656, and 57 days of the lunar year concurrent with the solar year 1657. A year of commensuration is always followed by a year of coincidence.

The sun was appointed for the measurement of time or years. The moon for the regulation and determination of the periodic returns of the "seasons," i.e. the set feasts and solemn assemblies... ("And God said, Let there be lights in the firmament of the heaven to divide the day from the night; and let them be for signs, and for seasons, and for days, and years. . ." Gen. 1:14 with "He appointed the moon for seasons: the sun knoweth his going down." Psa. 104:19)

Moses tables of the Patriarchs, like "Ptolemy's Canon of Kings", are constructed on astronomical principles. The numbers taken collectively constitute an uninterrupted series of true, tropical solar years, and register with astronomic accuracy the number of solar revolutions from the Creation of Adam to the death of Joseph, which no Chronologer who accepts the statements of the Hebrew Text can make either one year more, or one year less than 2369. Adam lived 930 years. The first year of his life runs parallel with Anno Hominis 1. The year in which he died runs parallel with Anno Hominis 930. Seth was born in the 130th year of Adam's life, the year Anno Hominis 130. It is not suggested that the Patriarchs were all born at the Autumnal Equinox or all on the same day of the same month of the year. The years are integral and take no account of fractions. The year of Seth's birth is reckoned to Adam. The 131st year of Adam's life, the year Anno Hominis 131 is reckoned as the first year of the life of Seth. Hence we may safely conclude that Moses' reckoning of years is inclusive, and Noah is said to be 600 years old at the beginning, and not the end of his 600th year.

The usual chronological statements of the years of the Kings reckon quite accurately in whole years, without introducing fractions of a year. For these whole years are always calendar years from New Year's Day (Nisan 1st) to New Year's Day. They are not measured from the day of the King's accession to the day of his death. They are designed like the years of the Patriarchs in Genesis, and the reigns of the Kings in Ptolemy's Canon, and in the Assyrian Eponym Canon, to mark the succession of the years in a given chronological Era.

It is not so with a chronological statement which contains fractions of a year like this of David's 7 1/2 years in Hebron. Here we have a statement measuring the exact duration of David's reign in Hebron, as measured from the day of his accession to the day of his removal to Jerusalem. When the statement is reproduced in terms of calendar years in 1 Chron. 29:27, the number assigned to David's reign is not 41 but 40 years. This is confirmed by the 480 years of 1 Kings 6:1, for if we give David 41 years, that figure would have to be altered to 481. We could not make David's reign 41 years in that list and still retain the number 480 by reducing the Joshua-Judges chasm to 12 instead of 13, for if we did that we should reduce Jephthah's 300 to 299. These numbers are so locked and inter- locked, so checked and doubly checked, that it is next to impossible to "correct" any one of them without throwing the whole system into confusion.[5]

The following table by Martin Anstey takes us from the flood to the birth of Abram:[6]

POSTDILUVIAN PATRIARCHS

From the Flood to the Birth of Abram.
AN. HOM.

1656	**The Flood** - Shem aged 98 (Gen. 11:10)
2	Add the years after the Flood when Arphaxad was born (Gen. 11:10)
1658	Arphaxad born. Shem aged 100.
35	Add age of Arphaxad at birth of Salah (Gen. 11:12)
1693	Salah born.
30	Add age of Salah at birth of Eber (Gen. 11:14).
1723	Eber born.
34	Add age of Eber at birth of Peleg (Gen. 11:16).
1757	Peleg born.
30	Add age of Peleg at birth of Reu (Gen. 11:18)
1787	Reu born.
32	Add age of Reu at birth of Serug (Gen. 11:20)
1819	Serug born.
30	Add age of Serug at birth of Nahor (Abram's grandfather) (Gen. 11:22).
1849	Nahor, Abram's grandfather, born.
29	Add age of Nahor at birth of Terah (Gen. 11:24).
1878	Terah born.
130	Add age of Terah at birth of Abram (Gen. 11:26,32, Gen. 12:4, Acts 7:4).
2008	**Abram born.**

The design of this genealogical list is to carry forward the Chronology from the date of the Flood to the birth of Abram.

Chapter 6
SEEING DAY 3

Abram to Samuel (about 1,000 years)

And the scripture, foreseeing that God would justify the heathen through faith, preached before the gospel unto Abraham, saying, In thee shall all nations be blessed.
—Galatians 3:8

Martin Anstey gives us some insight on the beginning of this time period:

> The Chronology of the remaining portion of Genesis is given on the same principles as that of the first eleven chapters. It follows the line of Abraham, through Isaac and Jacob and Joseph. As it is with the ante-diluvian and the post-diluvian Patriarchs, so it is with the Hebrew Patriarchs. The method adopted for measuring the time is that of giving the age of the father at the birth of his son, until we reach the name of Joseph. The age of Jacob at the birth of Joseph is nowhere directly stated, but it can be ascertained by an arithmetical calculation, or a historical induction. Abraham was born when Terah was 130, in the year AN. HOM. 2008. When Terah died, at the age of 205, Abraham left Haran, in obedience to the call of God, at the age of 75, in the year AN. HOM. 2083 (Gen. 11:32, 12:1, Acts 7:4).[1]

And Terah lived seventy years, and begat Abram, Nahor, and Haran. Now these are the generations of Terah: Terah begat Abram, Nahor, and Haran; and Haran begat Lot. And Haran died before his father Terah in the land of his nativity, in Ur of the Chaldees. And Abram and Nahor took them wives: the name of Abram's wife was Sarai; and the name of Nahor's wife, Milcah, the daughter of Haran, the father of Milcah, and the father of Iscah. But Sarai was barren; she had no child. And Terah took Abram his son, and Lot the son of Haran his son's son, and Sarai his daughter in law, his son Abram's wife; and they went forth with them from Ur of the Chaldees, to go into the land of Canaan; and they came unto Haran, and dwelt there. And the days of Terah were two hundred and five years: and Terah died in Haran.

—Genesis 11:26–32

Now the Lord had said unto Abram, Get thee out of thy country, and from thy kindred, and from thy father's house, unto a land that I will shew thee.

—Genesis 12:1

God Is a Covenant-Making and Covenant-Keeping God

The Bible reveals that God is a covenant-making, covenant-keeping and covenant-revealing God. The Bible itself is a covenantal book being divided into two sections, the Old and New Testaments (Covenants) and containing a progressive revelation of nine major covenants. These covenants comprise the purposes of God in both Creation and Redemption and involve time and eternity.[2]

Abrahamic Covenant

> After these things the word of the LORD came unto Abram in a vision, saying, Fear not, Abram: I am thy shield, and thy exceeding great reward. And Abram said, LORD God, what wilt thou give me, seeing I go childless, and the steward of my house [is] this Eliezer of Damascus? And Abram said, Behold, to me thou hast given no seed: and, lo, one born in my house is mine heir. And, behold, the word of the LORD came unto him, saying, This shall not be thine heir; but he that shall come forth out of thine own bowels shall be thine heir. And he brought him forth abroad, and said, Look now toward heaven, and tell the stars, if thou be able to number them: and he said unto him, So shall thy seed be. And he believed in the LORD; and he counted it to him for righteousness. And he said unto him, I am the LORD that brought thee out of Ur of the Chaldees, to give thee this land to inherit it. And he said, LORD God, whereby shall I know that I shall inherit it? And he said unto him, Take me *an heifer of three years old*, and *a she goat of three years old*, and *a ram of three years old*, and *a turtledove*, and *a young pigeon*. And he took unto him all these, and divided them in the midst, and laid each piece one against another: but the birds divided he not.
>
> —GENESIS 15:1–10, EMPHASIS ADDED

> And when the fowls came down upon the carcases, Abram drove them away. And when the sun was going down, a deep sleep fell upon Abram; and, lo, an horror of great darkness fell upon him. And he said unto Abram, Know of a surety that thy seed shall be a stranger in a land that is not theirs, and shall serve them; and they shall afflict them four hundred years. And also that nation Egypt, whom they shall serve, will I judge: and afterward shall they come out with great substance... And it came to pass, that, when the sun went down, and it was dark, behold a smoking furnace, and a burning lamp that passed between those pieces. *In the same day the* LORD *made a covenant with Abram, saying, Unto thy seed have I given this land, from the river of Egypt unto the great river, the river Euphrates.*
>
> —GENESIS 15:11–14, 17–18, EMPHASIS ADDED

Abraham—Two Sons

> Tell me, you who desire to be under the law, do you not listen to the law? For it is written that Abraham had two sons, one by a slave woman and one by a free woman. But the son of the slave was born according to the flesh, while the son of the free woman was born through promise. Now this may be interpreted allegorically: these women are two covenants. One is from Mount Sinai, bearing children for slavery; she is Hagar. Now Hagar is Mount Sinai in Arabia; she corresponds to the present Jerusalem, for she is in slavery with her children. But the Jerusalem above is free, and she is our mother. For it is written, "Rejoice, O barren one who does not bear; break forth and cry aloud, you who are not in labor! For the children of the desolate one will be more than those of the one who has a husband." Now you, brothers, like Isaac, are children of promise. But just as at that time he who was born according to the flesh persecuted him who was born according to the Spirit, so also it is now. But what does the Scripture say? "Cast out the slave woman and her son, for the son of the slave woman shall not inherit with the son of the free woman." So, brothers, we are not children of the slave but of the free woman.
>
> —GALATIANS 4:21–31, ESV

Galatians 4 Allegory

Old Covenant (Moses)	New Covenant (Christ)	Scripture
Hagar	Sarah	Galatians 4:22
Ishmael	Isaac	Galatians 4:22, 23
Bondwoman	Freewoman	Galatians 4:23
Born "after the flesh"	Born "by Promise"	Galatians 4:23
Mt. Sinai / Jerusalem now	Mt. Zion (Jerusalem above)	Galatians 4:25, 26
Mosaic Covenant (the Law)	New Covenant (Grace)	Galatians 4:24 (Allegory)
Bondage/Enslaved	Freedom/free	Galatians 4:24-26
After the flesh	After the Spirit	Galatians 4:23, 29
Earthly(Jerusalem now)	Heavenly (Jerusalem above)	Galatians 4:25, 26
Disinherited/Not Heirs	Grace / Heirs of Promise	Galatians 4:30
Persecutes Heirs	Persecuted by Disinherited	Galatians 4:29, 30

From the time of Abraham we see his call, his obedience in faith, his marriage with Hagar (the "allegory" of Galatians chapter 4), his two wives (Sarah and Hagar), his two sons (Ishmael and Isaac), the miraculous birth of Isaac the child of promise, the offering of Isaac, and the seeking of a wife for Isaac in Mesopotamia. This is evidence of the Bible's Divine authorship. Genesis is a history covering two thousand three hundred and sixty-nine (2369) years, from the creation of Adam to the death of Joseph; yet the personal incidents in the lives of Abraham, Isaac and Jacob could not be realized until the work of Christ in redemption was fully revealed by the New Testament.

Progression of the Abrahamic Covenant Throughout Scripture

Old Testament

Genesis 12:1-4 (Call, promise, words of covenant) A.H. 2083
Genesis 15:13-14 (Seed to be afflicted 400 years) A.H. 2113
Exodus 2:24 (God remembers his covenant) A.H. 2513
Exodus 12:40, 41 (End of 430 years) A.H. 2513 (The Exodus)
Leviticus 26:14-39 (Penalty of Sins - Captivity) A.H. 2514
Leviticus 26:40-46 (Remedy for Sins) A.H. 2514
Isaiah 44:21- 45:13 Prophecy Concerning Cyrus A.H. 3589
Jeremiah 25:1-13 (70 Years Desolation) A.H. 3521 (4th Year of Jehoiakim)
Daniel 9:1-27 (Daniel's Prayer and Prophecy) A.H. 3587 "unto Messiah"

New Testament

Matthew 26:28 (Blood shed for many)
Luke 1:67-80 (Zacharias prophecy)
John 8:56 (Abraham sees Christ's day)
Romans 15:8-11 (Confirmed promises)
Galatians 3:7-18 (Covenant confirmed)
Hebrews 2:16 (Took on Him the Seed of Abraham)
Hebrews 9:28 (Sacrifice bore sins of many)
Hebrews 11:8, 9 (Abraham sojourns with Isaac & Jacob

2083	2513	3520	3589	4071	4075
Abrahamic Covenant	The Law The Exodus	Captivity Begins	Captivity Ends Decree of Cyrus **Beginning of Daniel's 70 Week Prophecy**	Baptism	Crucifixion

The chronology of the remaining portion of Genesis is given on the same principles as that of the first eleven chapters. It follows the line of Abraham through Isaac and Jacob and Joseph. As it is with the antediluvian and the postdiluvian Patriarchs, so it is with the Hebrew Patriarchs. The method adopted for measuring the time is that of giving the age of the father at the birth of his son, until we reach the name of Joseph. The age of Jacob at the birth of Joseph is nowhere directly stated, but it can be ascertained by an arithmetical calculation or a historical induction. We begin with the result reached in chapter 5. Abraham was born when Terah was 130, in the year AH 2008. When Terah died, at the age of 205, Abraham left Haran, in obedience to the call of God at the age of seventy-five, in the year AH 2083 (Gen. 11:32; 12:1; Acts 7:4).

> By faith Abraham, when he was called to go out into a place which he should after receive for an inheritance, obeyed; and he went out, not knowing whither he went. By faith *he sojourned in the land of promise, as in a strange country, dwelling in tabernacles with Isaac and Jacob*, the heirs with him of the same promise.
>
> —HEBREWS 11:8–9, EMPHASIS ADDED

That these three witnesses have the truth, the chronology itself proves: for from Abraham's entry into Canaan to the birth of Isaac was *twenty-five* years (AH 2083–AH 2108).

> So Abram departed, as the LORD had spoken unto him; and Lot went with him: and Abram was *seventy and five years old* when he departed out of Haran.
>
> —GENESIS 12:4, EMPHASIS ADDED

Isaac was *sixty* years old at the birth of Jacob. (AH 2108–AH 2168)

> And after that came his brother out, and his hand took hold on Esau's heel; and his name was called Jacob: and Isaac was *threescore years old* when she bare them.
>
> —GENESIS 25:26, EMPHASIS ADDED

And Jacob was *130* at his going down into Egypt (AH 2168–AH 2298).

> And Jacob said unto Pharaoh, The days of the years of my pilgrimage are *an hundred and thirty years*: few and evil have the days of the years of my life been, and have not attained unto the days of the years of the life of my fathers in the days of their pilgrimage.
>
> —GENESIS 47:9, EMPHASIS ADDED

The total of the three sums make 215 years. And then Jacob and his children having continued in Egypt 215 years more, the whole sum of 430 years is mathematically warranted. Martin Anstey lays it out clearly in the following chart.[3]

The Call, Promise, and Covenant of Abraham to the Exodus

"The sojourning of the children of Israel who sojourned in Egypt was 430 years." **Hebrew Text of Ex. 12:40** The LXX. and the Samaritan insert after Egypt the words **"and in the land of Canaan,"** and consequently read, "the sojourning of the children of Israel who sojourned **in Egypt and in the land of Canaan was 430 years."** The added words agree perfectly with the Hebrew, which is further elucidated, but in no way modified by them. **They correctly interpret the meaning of the Hebrew Text**, and the fact that the interpretation put upon it is correct is shown by its adoption by Stephen (Acts 7:6) and by the Apostle Paul (Gal. 3:17). But the meaning of the Hebrew is sufficiently clear without the explanatory addition when the Text is properly translated. "And God spake on this wise, That **his seed should sojourn in a strange land; and that they should bring them into bondage, and entreat them evil four hundred years.**" Acts 7:6
"And this I say, that the covenant, that was confirmed before of God in Christ, **the law, which was four hundred and thirty years after**, cannot disannul, that it should make the promise of none effect." Galatians 3:17 **(Study Martin Anstey's chart below which shows a breakdown of the sojourn in Canaan and affliction in Egypt.)**

130 THE ROMANCE OF BIBLE CHRONOLOGY.

DIAGRAM OF THE 215, THE 400 AND THE 430 YEARS

OF SOJOURN IN CANAAN, AND THE SOJOURN AND AFFLICTION IN EGYPT.

Call, Promise and Covenant of Abraham. 2083.	Weaning of Isaac, who becomes Abraham's Seed and Heir. Ishmael disinherited. 2113	Jacob goes down into Egypt. 2298.	The Exodus and the giving of the Law. 2513.
30 years.	185 years.	215 years.	
Abraham sojourns in Canaan.	Abraham's Seed sojourn in Canaan	The Children of Israel sojourn and are afflicted in Egypt.	

The 215 years of Josephus, the LXX. and the Samaritan Version.

The 400 years of Genesis 15^{13} and Acts 7^{6}.

The 430 years of Exodus $12^{40, 41}$ and Galatians 3^{17}.

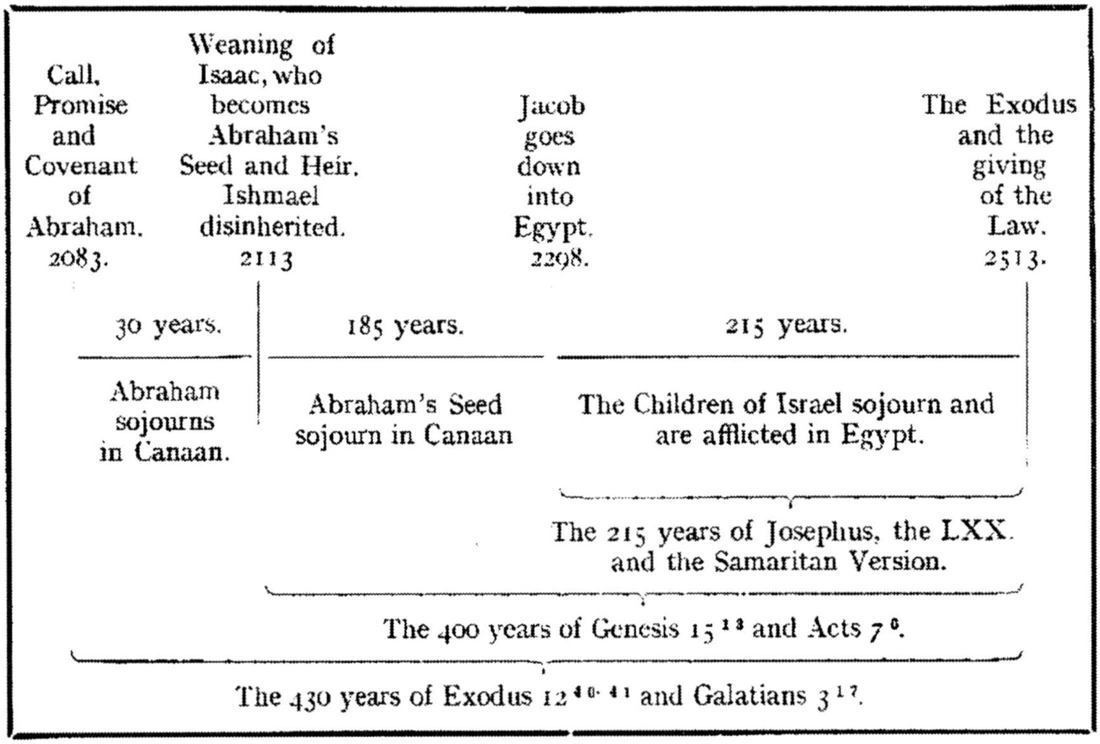

The following chart is an overview of years from the birth of Abram to the death of Joseph, and then computes the years from the Abrahamic Covenant to the Exodus.

THE BIRTH OF ABRAHAM TO THE DEATH OF JOSEPH

Abram	Isaac	Jacob	Joseph	Moses	The Law The Exodus
2008	2108	2168	2259-2369	2433	2513

"the sojourning of Abraham and his seed"
The 430 Years -- "the Law 430 years **after**"

2083
Abram's Call the Promise, and Covenant

Exodus 12:40,41; Galatians 3:17; Exodus 19:1,2

"his seed should sojourn. . .four hundred years"

2113
Isaac - Heir

Genesis 15:13; Acts 7:6; Galatians 3:29-4:5

2083	2093	2094	2107	2108	2113	2148	2168	2183
Abram's Call, Promise, Covenant.	Abram's marriage to Hagar.	Ishmael born.	Isaac Promised.	Isaac born.	Isaac becomes SEED/HEIR. Ishmael cast out.	Isaac married Age 40.	Birth of Esau & Jacob	Abraham's Death

286 YEARS FROM ABRAM'S CALL TO DEATH OF JOSEPH

2245	2252	2259	2265	2289	2296	2298	2315	2369
Jacob goes to Padan-Aram Jacob 77	Jacob marries Leah and Rachael at same time. Jacob 84	Joseph born. Jacob 91.	Jacob returns to Canaan. Jacob 97	Joseph stands before Pharaoh Joseph 30	Seven years of plenty. Joseph 37	Jacob goes down to Egypt Jacob 130	Jacob's Death (Age 147)	Joseph's Death Joseph 110

2369 Death of Joseph at 110
2083 <u>Call of Abraham at 75</u>
286 Years

2083 Abrahamic Covenant (Start of 430 years of Exodus 12:40-41 and Galatians 3:17)
<u>30</u> Add 30 years Abraham sojourns in Canaan.
2113 Great Feast, Isaac becomes Abraham's SEED and HEIR; Ishmael disinherited.
(Start of the 400 years of Genesis 15:13 and Acts 7:6)

<u>185</u> Abraham's SEED sojourn in Canaan
2298 Jacob goes down into Egypt (Start of 215 years of Josephus, the LXX, and Samaritan Version)

<u>215</u> Add 215 years The Children of Israel sojourn and are afflicted in Egypt.
2513 The Exodus and the giving of the Law. End of 430 years, 400 years, and 215 years.

2369	+64	2433	+40	2473	+40	**2513**
Joseph's Death		Moses birth.		Moses' flight.		**The Exodus and giving of the Law**

(144 total years)

Exodus 1:6–12:41, from the death of Joseph (AH 2369) to the Exodus (AH 2513), covers a period of 144 years. It is definitely stated that Moses was eighty years old when he and Aaron spoke to Pharaoh; and as the narrative is continuous, with no note of time to indicate anything to the contrary, we may conclude that the ten plagues all took place immediately afterwards, and that the Exodus was accomplished that same year. This is confirmed by the fact that one and one-half months before the completion of the forty years in the wilderness Moses died at the age of 120 years.

It is not definitely stated in the text of the Old Testament that Moses was exactly forty years old at the date of his flight, but we are told in Exodus 2:11 that it took place "when Moses was grown," a phrase, which at that time meant "when Moses was forty years of age," just as with us the phrase "coming of age" means arriving at the age of twenty-one. This is the interpretation put upon the words by Stephen in Acts 7:23, and on this point he is a credible authority. "And when he was full forty years old, it came into his heart to visit his brethren the children of Israel" (Acts 7:23).

But even if we were doubtful as to whether Moses fled to Midian exactly at the age of forty and led the people out of Egypt at the age of eighty, the date of the Exodus would be unaffected by the doubt and only two intermediate steps in the chronological ladder would be moved up or down with compensation elsewhere to bring *the Exodus* down to the year *AH 2513*. The following table by Martin Anstey shows the timeline from the call of Abraham to the Exodus.[4]

The Joseph-Moses Connection

From the Death of Joseph to the Birth of Moses = 64 years.

2369. Death of Joseph at age of 110
Add 64 years to the birth of Moses, for,-

Ex. 12:40,41, Call of Abram to Exodus =	430 years

From Call of Abram to death of Joseph (AN.HOM. 2083-2369) =	286 years

Therefore, Death of Joseph to Exodus =	144 years
Ex. 2:23, Acts 7:29,30, Flight of Moses to Exodus, when Moses was 80 =	40 years
Therefore, Death of Joseph to flight of Moses, =	104 years
Ex. 2:11-15, Acts 7:23-29, Birth of Moses to Flight of Moses, =	40 years
64. Therefore, Death of Joseph to Birth of Moses =	64 years

2433. Moses born.

The Exodus of the Children of Israel under the Leadership of Moses

The Exodus of the children of Israel from the land of Egypt and their journey through the wilderness was over a period of *forty years*.

> After the number of days in which ye searched the Land, even *forty days*, each day for a year, shall ye bear your iniquities, even *forty years*, and ye shall know my breach of promise.
>
> —Numbers 14:34, emphasis added

All of the events occurring in the Book of Exodus lasted a period of *144 years and eleven and one-half months*, which was a brief time compared with the *2,369* years of the Book of Genesis (AH 1, the first year of Adam's life, unto AH 2369, the year of Joseph's death). The chronology of the Book of Leviticus is only *one month*. Compare the two scriptures:

> And it came to pass in the *first month in the second year, on the first day of the month*, that the tabernacle was reared up.
>
> —Exodus 40:17, emphasis added

> And the Lord spake unto Moses in the wilderness of Sinai, in the tabernacle of the congregation, on the *first day of the second month, in the second year* after they were come out of the land of Egypt.
>
> —Numbers 1:1, emphasis added

The numbering of the tribes of Israel as recorded in the Book of Numbers extended for *twenty days*:

> And it came to pass on the *twentieth day of the second month, in the second year*, that the cloud was taken up from off the tabernacle of the testimony. And the children of Israel took their journeys out of the wilderness of Sinai; and the cloud rested in the wilderness of Paran.
>
> —Numbers 10:11, emphasis added

So the time of the children of Israel's sojourn around Mt. Sinai was almost one year. Then at the wilderness of Paran, Moses sent the twelve heads of the children of Israel to spy out the land:

> And Moses by the commandment of the Lord sent them from the wilderness of Paran: all those men were heads of the children of Israel.
>
> —Numbers 13:3

However, because of the "majority's" *evil report* of the ten spies and due to unbelief of the people, they could not enter into the land of promise.

> For some, when they had heard, did provoke: howbeit not all that came out of Egypt by Moses. But with whom was he grieved forty years? was it not with them that had sinned, whose carcases fell in the wilderness? And to whom sware he that they should not enter into his rest, but to them that believed not? So we see that *they could not enter in because of unbelief.*
>
> —Hebrews 3:16–19, emphasis added

> Say unto them, As truly as I live, saith the LORD, as ye have spoken in mine ears, so will I do to you: Your carcases shall fall in this wilderness; and all that were numbered of you, according to your whole number, from twenty years old and upward, which have murmured against me.
>
> —NUMBERS 14:28–29

From this point in time, for a period of thirty-seven years and eleven months, there is no dated event in the journey of the children of Israel through the wilderness. The next dated event occurs with the death of Miriam.

> Then came the children of Israel, even the whole congregation, into the desert of Zin in the *first month*: and the people abode in Kadesh; and Miriam died there, and was buried there.
>
> —NUMBERS 20:1, EMPHASIS ADDED

> And they removed from Eziongaber, and pitched in the wilderness of Zin, which is Kadesh. And they removed from Kadesh, and pitched in mount Hor, in the edge of the land of Edom. And *Aaron* the priest went *up into mount Hor* at the commandment of the LORD, *and died there, in the fortieth year after the children of Israel were come out of the land of Egypt, in the first day of the fifth month.*
>
> —NUMBERS 33:36–38, EMPHASIS ADDED

In the "first month" that Miriam died was actually the first month of the fortieth year in the wilderness from the Exodus from Egypt. Therefore, thirty-eight years had passed since the last dated event. Moses no doubt died in the year AH 2553. There were thirty days of mourning for him on the plains of Moab.

> And the children of Israel wept for Moses in the plains of Moab *thirty days*: so the days of weeping and mourning for Moses were ended.
>
> —DEUTERONOMY 34:8, EMPHASIS ADDED

> And it came to pass after *three days*, that the officers went through the host.
>
> —JOSHUA 3:2, EMPHASIS ADDED

In the year AH 2553, month 1, day 14, the children of Israel encamped in Gilgal.

> And the children of Israel encamped in Gilgal, and kept the passover on the *fourteenth day of the month* at even in the plains of Jericho.
>
> —JOSHUA 5:10, EMPHASIS ADDED

Moses was a hundred and twenty years old when he died.

> And Moses was *an hundred and twenty years old* when he died: his eye was not dim, nor his natural force abated.
>
> —DEUTERONOMY 34:7, EMPHASIS ADDED

Moses was born AH 2433 and he was in his one hundred and twentieth year when he died in AH 2553.

The following chart by Martin Anstey gives the timeline from the entry into Canaan to the division of the land.[5]

The Seven Years' War
(*Martin Anstey*)

From the Entry into Canaan to the Division of the Land.

(AN. HOM. **2553-2560**).

AN. HOM.
2553. The entry into Canaan
Add 7 years to division of the Land, for:-

Exodus (Ex. 12:40,41)	= **2513**
Spies sent out in 2nd year after the Exodus (Numb. 10:11,12; 13:17-20)	= **2515**

At that date Caleb was **40** (Josh. 14:7)

Therefore, Caleb was born **2515 - 40**	= **2475**

But at the division of the Land Caleb was **85** (Josh. 14:10).

Therefore, division of the Land took place in **2475+85**	= **2560**

7. Therefore, from entry of Canaan to division of Land = **2560 - 2553 = 7 years**
2560. Division of the Land at end of Seven Years' War.

The following chart for "Day 3" shows the 400 and the 430 years from Abraham to the Law of Moses, the breakdown of the 594 years from the Exodus to the fourth year of Solomon's reign, the 480 years of 1 Kings 6:1, and the 450 years of Acts 15:20.

DIAGRAM OF DAY 3

Diagram Showing the 400 and 430 years from Abraham to the Law of Moses And the Breakdown of the 594 years from the Exodus to the 4th year of Solomon's Reign, the 480 years of I Kings 6:1, and the 450 years of Acts 13:20

Abram	Isaac	Jacob	Joseph	Moses	The Law The Exodus	Wilderness Wanderings	Seven Years War	Division of Land to Judges	Period of the Judges
2008	2108	2168	2259-2369	2433	2513	2513-2553	2553-2560	2560-2573	2573-3023

"the sojourning of Abraham and his seed"
The 430 Years -- "the Law 430 years **after**"

2083
Abram's Call the Promise, and Covenant
Exodus 12:40,41; Galatians 3:17; Exodus 19:1,2

"his seed should sojourn. . .four hundred years"
The 400 Years

2113
Issac - Heir
Genesis 15:13; Acts 7:6; Galatians 3:29-4:5

1 Kings 6:1
2513-3106 = 594 Total Years
480 Theocratic Years

"And after that he gave unto them judges about the space of 450 years"
Acts 13:20

Exodus to 4th Year of Solomon

40	The Wanderings
7	Seven Years War
13	Division of Land to Oppression
450	Period of the Judges
40	Saul
40	David
4	Solomon
594	Total Years unto 4th Year of Solomon's Reign
- 114	Non-Theocratic Years*
480	**Theocratic Years**

Period of the Judges

8	Cushan*
40	**Othniel**
18	Eglon*
80	**Ehud**
20	Jabin*
40	**Barak**
7	Midian*
40	**Gideon**
3	Abimelech*
23	**Tola**
22	**Jair**
18	Ammon*
6	**Jephthah**
7	**Ibzan**
10	**Elan**
8	**Abdon**
40	Philistines*
40	**Eli**
20	**Samuel**
450	**Total Years**

The following chronology by Martin Anstey gives a detailed timeline of the period of the judges.[6]

Chronology of the Period of the Judges

A.H. 2573. 1st Servitude, under Cushan.

8. Add 8 years' Servitude under Cushan (Jud. 3:8).

> "Therefore the anger of the LORD was hot against Israel, and he sold them into the hand of Chushanrishathaim king of Mesopotamia: and the children of Israel served Chushanrishathaim **eight years**." Judges 3:8

A.H. 2581. Rest by Othniel.

40. Add 40 years' Rest by Othniel

> "And the land had rest **forty years**. And Othniel the son of Kenaz died. Judges 3:11

A.H. 2631. 2nd Servitude, under Eglon.

18. Add 18 years' Servitude under Eglon.

> "So the children of Israel served Eglon the king of Moab **eighteen years**." Judges 3:14

A.H. 2639. Rest by Ehud.

Judgeship of Shamgar (Jud. 3:31) included in **20 years** of 3rd Servitude, under Jabin (Jud. 5:6,7).

> "And after him was Shamgar the son of Anath, which slew of the Philistines six hundred men with an ox goad: and he also delivered Israel." Judges 3:31

> "In the days of Shamgar the son of Anath, in the days of Jael, the highways were unoccupied, and the travellers walked through byways." [The inhabitants of] the villages ceased, they ceased in Israel, until that I Deborah arose, that I arose a mother in Israel." Judges 5:6,7

80. Add 80 years' Rest by Ehud.

> "So Moab was subdued that day under the hand of Israel. And the land had rest **fourscore years**." Judges 3:30

A.H. 2719. 3rd Servitude, under Jabin.

20. Add 20 years' Servitude under Jabin.

> "And the children of Israel cried unto the LORD: for he had nine hundred chariots of iron; and **twenty years** he mightily oppressed the children of Israel." Judges 4:3

A.H. 2739. Rest by Barak.

40. Add 40 years' Rest by Barak

> "So let all thine enemies perish, O LORD: but let them that love him be as the sun when he goeth forth in his might. And the land had rest **forty years**." Judges 5:31

A.H. 2779. 4th Servitude, under Midian.

7. Add 7 years' Servitude under Midian.

> "And the children of Israel did evil in the sight of the LORD: and the LORD delivered them into the hand of Midian **seven years**." Judges 6:1

A.H. 2786. Rest by Gideon.

40. Add 40 years' Rest by Gideon

> "Thus was Midian subdued before the children of Israel, so that they lifted up their heads no more. And the country was in quietness **forty years** in the days of Gideon." Judges 8:28

A.H. 2826. Usurpation by Abimelech.

3. Add 3 years' Usurpation of Abimelech.

"When Abimelech had reigned **three years** over Israel," Judges 9:22

A.H. 2829. Judgeship of Tola.

23. Add 23 years' Judgeship of Tola.

> "And after Abimelech there arose to defend Israel Tola the son of Puah, the son of Dodo, a man of Issachar; and he dwelt in Shamir in mount Ephraim. And he judged Israel **twenty and three years**, and died, and was buried in Shamir." Judges 10:1,2

A.H. 2852. Judgeship of Jair.

22. Add 22 years' Judgeship of Jair.

> "And after him arose Jair, a Gileadite, and judged Israel **twenty and two years**." Judges 10:3

A.H. 2874. 5th Servitude, under Ammon.

18. Add 18 years' Servitude under Ammon.

"And that year they vexed and oppressed the children of Israel: **eighteen years**, all the children of Israel that were on the other side Jordan in the land of the Amorites, which is in Gilead." Judges 10:8

A.H. 2892. Judgeship of Jephthah.

6. Add 6 years' Judgeship of Jephthah.

"And Jephthah judged Israel six years. Then died Jephthah the Gileadite, and was buried in one of the cities of Gilead." Judges 12:7

A.H. 2898. Judgeship of Ibzan.

7. Add 7 years' Judgeship of Ibzan.

"And after him Ibzan of Bethlehem judged Israel. And he had thirty sons, and thirty daughters, whom he sent abroad, and took in thirty daughters from abroad for his sons. And he judged Israel **seven years**." Judges 12:8,9

A.H. 2905. Judgeship of Elon.

10. Add 10 years' Judgeship of Elon.

"And after him Elon, a Zebulonite, judged Israel; and he judged Israel **ten years**." Judges 12:11

A.H. 2915. Judgeship of Abdon.

8. Add 8 years' Judgeship of Abdon.

"And he had forty sons and thirty nephews, that rode on threescore and ten ass colts: and he judged Israel eight years." Judges 12:14

A.H. 2923. 6th Servitude, under the Philistines.

Judgeship of **Samson 20 years** (Jud. 16:31) included in 40 years of 6th Servitude, under Philistines.

"And Samson said, Let me die with the Philistines. And he bowed himself with all his might; and the house fell upon the lords, and upon all the people that [were] therein. So the dead which he slew at his death were more than [they] which he slew in his life. Then his brethren and all the house of his father came down, and took him, and brought him up, and buried him between Zorah and Eshtaol in the buryingplace of Manoah his father. And he judged Israel **twenty years**." Judges 16:30,31

"And he judged Israel in the days of the Philistines **twenty years**." Judges 15:20

40. Add 40 years' Servitude under Philistines.

"And the children of Israel did evil again in the sight of the LORD; and the LORD delivered them into the hand of the Philistines forty years." Judges 13:1

A.H. 2963. Judgeship of Eli.

40. Add 40 years' Judgeship of Eli.

"And it came to pass, when he made mention of the ark of God, that he fell from off the seat backward by the side of the gate, and his neck brake, and he died: for he was an old man, and heavy. And he had judged Israel **forty years**." 1 Samuel 4:18

A.H. 3003. Judgeship of Samuel.

20. Add 20 years' Judgeship of Samuel, 1 Sam. 7:2 (1 Sam. 7:13-17 is a review, not a continuation of the history).

> "And it came to pass, while the ark abode in Kirjathjearim, that the time was long; for it was **twenty years**: and all the house of Israel lamented after the LORD." 1 Samuel 7:2

> "So the Philistines were subdued, and they came no more into the coast of Israel: and the hand of the LORD was against the Philistines all the days of Samuel. And the cities which the Philistines had taken from Israel were restored to Israel, from Ekron even unto Gath; and the coasts thereof did Israel deliver out of the hands of the Philistines. And there was peace between Israel and the Amorites. And Samuel judged Israel all the days of his life. And he went from year to year in circuit to Bethel, and Gilgal, and Mizpeh, and judged Israel in all those places. And his return was to Ramah; for there was his house; and there he judged Israel; and there he built an altar unto the LORD." 1 Samuel 7:13-17

In the following table, Martin Anstey covers the condition of Israel during the period from Cushan to Saul.[7]

Israel under the Judges

From the 1st Servitude under Cushan to the Election of Saul

Periods	Servitude	Rest	Usurpation	Judgeship
1st Servitude, under Cushan	8	*	*	*
Rest by Othniel	*	40	*	*
2nd Servitude, under Eglon	18	*	*	*
Rest by Ehud	*	80	*	*
(Judgeship of Shamgar included in 3rd Servitude				*
under Jabin. Judges 3:31 - 5:6,7	*	*	*	*
3rd Servitude, under Jabin	20	*	*	*
Rest by Barak	*	40	*	*
4th Servitude, under Midian	7	*	*	*
Rest by Gideon	*	40	*	*
Usurpation of Abimelech	*	*	3	*
Judgeship of Tola	*	*	*	23
Judgeship of Jair	*	*	*	22
5th Servitude, under Ammon	18	*	*	*
Judgeship of Jephthah	*	*	*	6
Judgeship of Ibzan	*	*	*	7
Judgeship of Elon	*	*	*	10
Judgeship of Abdon	*	*	*	8
6th Servitude, under the Philistines	40	*	*	*
(Judgeship of Samson included in 6th Servitude,	*	*	*	*
under the Philistines, Judges 15:20	*	*	*	*
Judgeship of Eli	*	*	*	40
Judgeship of Samuel	*	*	*	20
(N. B. -- 1 Samuel 7:13-17 is a Review, not a continuation of the history)				
Totals	111	200	3	136

THE WHOLE PERIOD OF THE JUDGES.

Years of Servitude	111
Years of Rest	200
Years of Usurpation	3
Years of Judgeship	136
[TOTAL]	450

THE JUDGES INCLUDING SAMUEL = 450 YEARS.

THE Table above exhibits the Chronology of the period of the Judges, from the 1st servitude under Cushan to the election of Saul. The years of servitude, rest, usurpation, and Judgeship, are set out in four different columns, and it will be seen that the four totals amount to exactly 450 years. St. Paul, in his address at Antioch in Pisidia, says: "He divided their land to them by lot. And after that he gave unto them Judges about the space of 450 years until (heos = up to and including) Samuel the Prophet." Acts 13:19,20. Here again the minutest accuracy is observed.

It will be seen that the number of the years from the oppression of Cushan to the end of Samuel's Judgeship is not "about," but exactly 450 years. St. Paul is, however, quite right in using the word "about," and he was compelled to use it in order to be accurate, because the period of which he is speaking is the period from the division of the Land to the end of the judgeship of Samuel. It includes, therefore, the so-called Joshua - Judges chasm of 13 years, and as this is not specified in the Text of the Old Testament, and not included in the 450 years that are specified, St. Paul is obliged to allow for this space, and he does so quite naturally and quite accurately by describing this period as a period of "about 450 years."

Table from Martin Anstey's "Romance of Bible Chronology"

The God of this people of Israel chose our fathers, and exalted the people when they dwelt as strangers in the land of Egypt, and with an high arm brought he them out of it. And about the time of forty years suffered he their manners in the wilderness. And when he had destroyed seven nations in the land of Chanaan, he divided their land to them by lot. And after that he gave unto them judges about *the space of four hundred and fifty years, until* [up to and including] *Samuel the prophet*. And afterward they desired a king: and God gave unto them Saul the son of Cis, a man of the tribe of Benjamin, by the space of forty years. And when he had removed him, he raised up unto them David to be their king; to whom also he gave testimony, and said, I have found David the son of Jesse, a man after mine own heart, which shall fulfil all my will.

—Acts 13:17–22, emphasis added

Chapter 7
SEEING DAY 4

Samuel to Christ (about 1,000 years)

And all the prophets who have spoken, from Samuel and those who came after him, also proclaimed these days. You are the sons of the prophets and of the covenant that God made with your fathers, saying to Abraham, "And in your offspring shall all the families of the earth be blessed." God, having raised up his servant, sent him to you first, to bless you by turning every one of you from your wickedness.
—Acts 3:24–26, esv

Day 4 (From Samuel to Christ) Overview

Samuel was the key man between the period of the judges of Israel and the prophets and kings of the United Kingdom of Israel which duration lasted 120 years (Saul, David, and Solomon each reigned for forty years). Samuel was Israel's last judge and he anointed the first two kings of Israel, Saul and David (AH 3023 and AH 3063). He was a priest, judge, and prophet who ushered in and unified all the geographically separated tribes of Israel into a united kingdom.

Israel had rejected the theocratic rule of God during the period of the judges and desired a king like the other nations surrounding them. Of the Northern Kingdom (Israel) out of the *twenty kings* there were *none righteous* that reigned. They had prophets assigned to them by God (Elijah, Elisha, Jonah, Amos, Hosea, and Micah). The two southern tribes (Judah and Benjamin) had prophets assigned to them (Joel, Isaiah, Micah, Nahum, Zephaniah, Habakkuk, Jeremiah, Ezekiel, and Daniel). Of the Kingdom of Judah (the two southern tribes) there were *eight righteous kings* of the *twenty kings* that reigned (Asa, Jehoshaphat, Joash, Amaziah, Uzziah, Jotham, Hezekiah, and Josiah).

After the kingship of Solomon had ended in AH 3143, the United Kingdom was divided into the Northern Kingdom (called Israel) and the Southern Kingdom (called Judah). The Kingdom of Israel's (N.K.) duration was from AH 3143 unto AH 3406 or *263 years*. The Kingdom of Judah's (S.K.) duration was from AH 3143 unto AH 3539 or *396 years*. The *Northern Kingdom* went into *Assyrian captivity* at its conclusion, and the *Southern Kingdom* went into *Babylonian captivity* at its conclusion. The Babylonian captivity lasted seventy years (AH 3520–AH 3589), fulfilling Jeremiah's prophecy (Jer. 25:11). (See "The Kings and Prophets of Judah and Israel" chart.)

At the conclusion of the seventy-year Babylonian captivity, *Cyrus*, king of Persia, made a decree in AH 3589, according to the prophecy in Daniel chapter 9, to release the people to return to their land and to restore and build Jerusalem and build the temple. (See Isaiah 44:28 and 45:1, 13.) The first *seven weeks* (or forty-nine years) of Daniel's seventy weeks prophecy was the period of "troublous times" (during the times of Ezra, Nehemiah, Haggai, Zechariah, and Malachi) from AH 3589 to AH 3637, which ends with the prophecy of Malachi and the close of the Old Testament. (*Inclusive*

Reasoning tells us: including the first year of the reign of Cyrus unto the end of the Old Testament is forty-nine total years.)

From AH 3637 unto AH 4071 fulfilled the *sixty-two weeks* (or 434 years), when John the Baptist baptized Jesus in the river Jordan and Andrew told Peter, "We have found Messias" (John 1:41). These events are laid out clearly on the following diagram. AH 4071 was AD 26. Jesus was crucified just three and one-half years (or one-half week) later in AD 30.

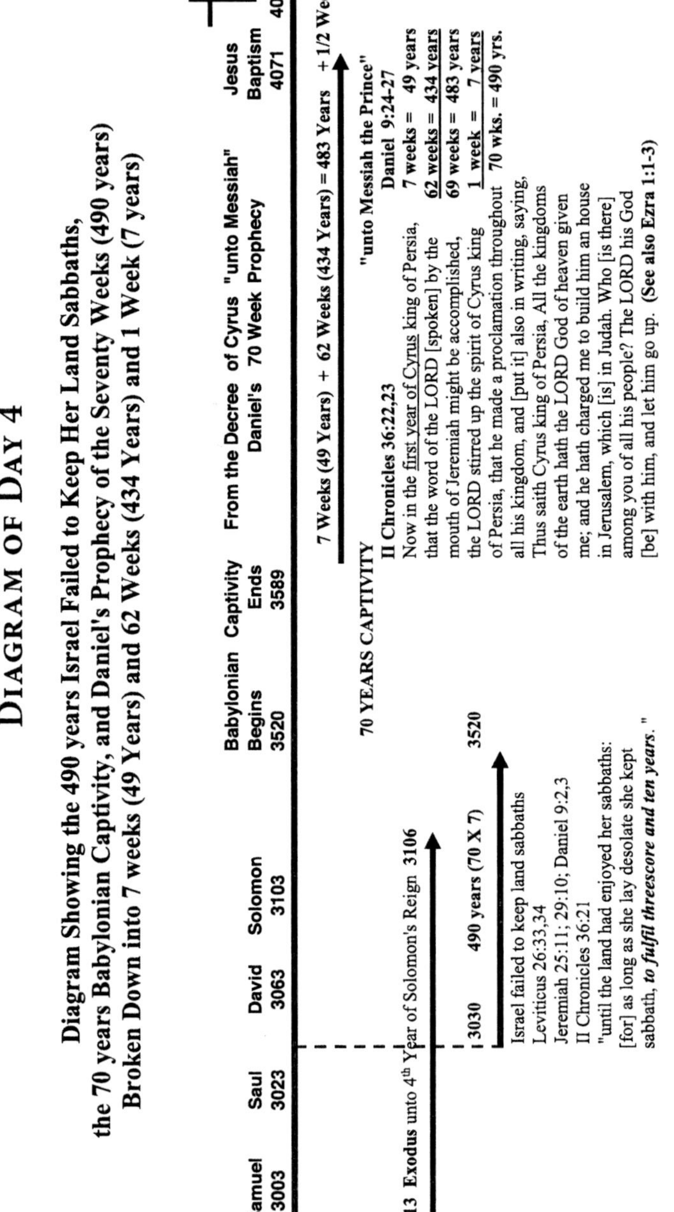

The following table of chronological events from Adam to Christ uses Bible-dated events based on Martin Anstey's *Chronology of the Old Testament* and Philip Mauro's *Wonders of Bible Chronology.*[1]

Chronology of the Old Testament

Event	A.H.	B.C.	
Day 1			
Adam created	**1**	**4046**	
Adam's age at birth of Seth	130	3916	
Add Seth's age at birth of Enos (105)	235	3811	
Add Enos' age at birth of Cainan (90)	325	3721	
Add Cainan's age at birth of Mahalaleel (70)	395	3651	
Add Mahalaleel's age at birth of Jared (65)	460	3586	
Add Jared's age at birth of Enoch (162)	622	3424	
Add Enoch's age at birth of Methuselah (65)	687	3359	
Add Methuselah's age at birth of Lamech (187)	874	3172	
Day 2			
Add Lamech's age at **birth of Noah** (182)	**1056**	**2990**	
Add Noah's age at the time of the Flood (600)	1056	2390	
The Flood	**1656**	**2390**	
Add two years to birth of Arphaxad	1658	2388	
Add age of Arphaxad at birth of Salah (35)	1693	2353	
Add age of Salah at birth of Eber (30)	1723	2323	
Add age of Eber at birth of Peleg (34)	1757	2289	
Add age of **Peleg** at birth of Reu (30) **"in his days was the earth divided"**	1787	2259	
Add age of Reu at birth of Serug (32)	1819	2227	
Add age of Serug at birth of Nahor (30)	1849	2197	
Add age of Nahor at birth of Terah (29)	1878	2168	
Day 3			
Birth of Abram	**2008**	**2038**	
Abram's call, promise, covenant (*Gen* 12:1-3, 15:13-18, *Gal*.3:17)	2083	1963	
Abram's marriage with Hagar (*Gen.* 16.3)	2093	1953	
Ishmael born (*Gen.* 16:16)	2094	1952	
Isaac promised	2107	1939	
Isaac born	**2108**	**1938**	

Explanatory Notes: AN. HOM. = ANNO HOMINIS = The year of the Era of Man, reckoning from the year of the Creation of Adam onward.
B.C. = The year of the Era before Christ.

Event	A.H.	B.C.	
Isaac becomes Abraham's SEED & HEIR (Gen. 15:13; 21:8-10; Acts 7:6)	**2113**	**1933**	
Ishmael cast out (Gen.21:10; Gal. 3:29-4:5)	2113	1933	
Death of Sarah at 127 (Gen. 23:1) Sarah is the only woman with age given in Scriptures	2145	1901	
Isaac married at age of 40 (Gen. 25:20)	2148	1898	
Birth of Esau and **Jacob**	**2168**	**1878**	
Abraham's death (Gen. 25:7, age 175)	2183	1863	
Esau's marriage (Gen. 26:34, age 40)	2208	1838	
Jacob goes to Padan Aram, aged 77	2245	1801	
Jacob marries Leah & Rachael at the same time (Gen. 29:21-30)	2252	1794	
Joseph born 7 years later (Gen. 30:25-26; 31:38-41) Jacob was 91	2259	1787	
Jacob returns to Canaan (Gen. 31:41) age 97	2265	1781	
Joseph stands before Pharoah (Gen. 41:46) age 30	**2289**	**1757**	
Add 7 years of plenty, Joseph 37	2296	1750	
Jacob goes down to Egypt (Gen. 45:6,47:9) at 130	2298	1748	
Death of Jacob 17 years later (Gen. 47:28)	2315	1731	
Death of Joseph	**2369**	**1677**	
Birth of Moses (add 64 years)	**2433**	**1613**	
Flight of Moses from Egypt (Ex. 2:11-15)	2473	1573	
Birth of **Caleb** (Josh. 14:7; 14:10)	**2475**	**1571**	
Return of Moses and the Exodus (Exodus 12:40-41; Gal. 3:17)	**2513**	**1533**	
Israel's arrival at Wilderness of Sin	2513	1533	
Giving of Manna and Smiting of the Rock	2513	1533	
The Exodus and the giving of the Law	**2513**	**1533**	
The Tabernacle of Moses built	2514	1532	
Numbering of Israel	2514	1532	
Spies sent forth	2514	1532	
Death of Miriam +38 yrs.	2552	1494	
Death of Aaron	2552	1494	
Defeat of Sihon & Og, Balaam & Balak, Numbering	2552	1494	

Explanatory Notes: AN. HOM. = ANNO HOMINIS = The year of the Era of Man, reckoning from the year of the Creation of Adam onward.
B.C. = The year of the Era before Christ.

Event	A.H.	B.C.		
Wilderness Wanderings End (2513-2553)/Moses died	2553	1493		
Entrance of Israel into Canaan (Numbers 13:20 with Josh. 14:7,10)	**2553**	**1493**		
Add 7 Years to **Division of Land** at end of **7 Years War** (Jos. 13:7-10)	2560	1486		
Add 13 years to oppression by Cushan (Jud. 3:8)	2573	1473		
Add 8 years from Cushan to Othniel (Jud. 3:8,11)	2581	1465		
Add 40 years to servitude under Eglon (Jud 3:11,14)	2621	1425		
Add 18 years to rest under Ehud (Jud. 3:14,30)	2639	1407		
Add 80 years to servitude under Jabin (Jud. 3:30)	2719	1327		
Add 20 years from Shamgar to Barak(Jud. 3:31;4:3)	2739	1307		
Add 40 years to servitude under *Midian* (Jud. 5:31)	2779	1267		
Add 7 years' servitude to rest by *Gideon* (Jud.6:1;8:28)	2786	1260		
Add 40 years' rest to Abimelech (Jud. 8:28; 9:22)	2826	1220		
Add 3 years' usurpation (Jud. 9:22) to Tola (Jud. 10:2)	2829	1217		
Add 23 years Tola to judgeship of Jair (Jud 10:2,3)	2852	1194		
Add 22 years to servitude under Ammon (Jud. 10:3,8)	2874	1172		
Add 18 years to the judgeship under Jephthah	2892	1154		
Add 6 years to Ibzan (Jud. 12:7)	2898	1148		
Add 7 years to Elon (Jud. 12:8,11)	2905	1141		
Add 10 years to Abdon (Jud. 12:11,14)	2915	1131		
Add 8 years to servitude under Philistines (Jud. 12:14)	2923	1123		
Add 40 years unto Eli (including Samson) (Jud. 16:31)	2963	1083		
Day 4			**Judah**	**Israel**
Add 40 years Eli's judgeship unto Samuel (1 Sam. 4:18)	**3003**	**1043**		
Add 20 years Samuel's judgeship to Saul (1 Sam. 7:2)	3023	1023		
Beginning of Saul's reign (Acts 13:21)	**3023**	**1023**	Saul	
Beginning of David's reign (2 Sam. 5:4,5; 2 Sam. 2:10	**3063**	**983**	David	
Beginning of Solomon's reign (2 Chr. 9:30)	**3103**	**943**	Solomon	
Death of Solomon. 10 tribes revolt. (1 K. 12;19,20,21)	3143	903	Rehoboam	Jeroboam
Add 17 years, reign of Rehoboam (1 Kings 11:43; 14:21)	3160	886		

Explanatory Notes: AN. HOM. = ANNO HOMINIS = The year of the Era of Man, reckoning from the year of the Creation of Adam onward.
B.C. = The year of the Era before Christ.

Event	A.H.	B.C.	Judah	Israel
Rehoboam died (1 K. 14:31)	3160	886		
Abijam reigned 3 years (1 K. 15:1,2)	3160	886	Abijam	
Abijam dies, succeeded by Asa (1 K. 15:9)	3163	883	Asa	
Nadab reigned over Israel 2nd year of Asa (1 K. 15:25)	3164	882		Nadab
Baasha reigned the3rd year of Asa (1 K. 15:28,33)	3165	881		Baasha
Great revival under Asa's reign (2 Chr. 15:1-10)	3177	869		
Baasha invaded Judah (2 Chr. 16:1)	3178	868		
Elah reigned the 26th year of Asa (1 K. 16:8)	3188	858		Elah
Zimri slew Elah & in turn was slain by Omri (1 K. 16:3,9,10)	3189	857		Omri/Tibni/Zimri
Omri and Tibni reign concurrently as rival kings	3189	857		
Tibni died. Omri continued to reign (1 K. 16:22,23)	3193	853		Omri
Omri made Samaria capital of his kingdom (1 K. 16:23,24)	3194	852		
Ahab succeeds Omri (1 K. 16:29)	3200	846		Ahab
Asa diseased in his feet (2 Chr. 16:12)	3201	845		
Asa dies, Jehoshaphat succeeds (2 Chr. 16:13; 1 K. 22:41,42)	3204	842	Jehoshaphat	
Jeshoshaphat sends forth princes & priests (2 Chr. 17:7-9)	3206	840		
Ahab slain in battle succeeded by Ahaziah (1 K. 22:37-40)	3220	826		Ahaziah
Jehoram reigns *for* Jehoshaphat (2 K.1:17 with 3:1) pro-Rex	3220	826	Jehoram/pro-Rex	
Elijah calls down fire from heaven (2 K. 1:9-12)	3220	826		
Ahaziah of Israel dies/Jehoram succeeds (2 K. 1:17; 3:1)	3221	825		Jehoram
Jehoram of Judah co-rex with Jehoshaphat (2 K. 8:16,17)	3225	821	Jehoram/co-Rex	
Jeshoshaphat died, and Jehoram sole king (1 K. 22:50)	3229	817	Jehoram/sole king	
Ahaziah joint reign with his father/co-Rex (2 K. 9:29)	3231	815	Ahaziah/co-Rex	
Ahaziah one year as sole king (2 K. 8:25,26)	3232	814	Ahaziah/sole king	
Jehu slays Ahaziah/Jehoram (2 K. 9:13-33; 10:36; 2 K. 11:1-4)	3233	813	Athaliah	Jehu
Athaliah slain in 7th year, succeeded by Joash (2 K. 12:1; 2 K. 11:4-16)	3239	807	Joash (Johash)	
Jehu reigned 28 years, succeeded by his son Jehoahaz (2 K. 13:1)	3261	785		Jehoahaz
Joash repairs the Temple (2 K. 12:6,7)	3261	785		
Jehoash reigned in Israel (co-Rex with Jehoahaaz (2 K. 13:9,10)	3275	771		Jehoash/co-Rex
Jehoahaz, king of Israel, died; Jehoash reigns as sole king (2 K. 13:9-10)	3278	768		Jehoash/sole king

Explanatory Notes: AN. HOM. = ANNO HOMINIS = The year of the Era of Man, reckoning from the year of the Creation of Adam onward.
B.C. = The year of the Era before Christ.

Event	A.H.	B.C.	Judah	Israel
Amaziah succeeded his father Joash (2 K. 12:21; 14:1,2)	3279	767	Amaziah	
Jeroboam II reigned as king of Israel (2 K. 14:16,23) 41 years	3293	753		Jeroboam II
Amaziah died (2 Kings 14:17) 15 years after death of Jehoash	3308	738		
An Interregnum - Judah had no king for 11 years	3308	738	Interregnum	
Uzziah begins to reign in 27th year of Jeroboam II (2 K. 14:21;15:1,2)	3319	727	Uzziah (or Azariah)	
After Jeroboam II, Israel had no king for 22 years	3334	712		Interregnum
Zechariah ascends to throne - 2 K. 14:29; 15:8) - Uzziah's 38th year	3356	690		Zechariah
Shallum reigns 1 month succeeded by Menahem (2 K. 15:10-17) reigns 10	3357	689		Shallum/Menahem
Jotham as judge last years of Uzziah (2 K. 15:5; 2 Chr. 26:21)	3367	679	Jotham (as Judge)	
Pekahiah reigns in 50th year of Uzziah (2 K. 15:22,23)	3368	678		Pekahiah
Pekah slays Pekahiah and reigns in his stead (2 K. 15:25-27)	3370	676		Pekah
Isaiah's great vision (Is. 6:1) and death of Uzziah	3371	675		
Jotham succeeds Uzziah in 2nd year of Pekah (2 K. 15:32,33)	3371	675	Jotham (as king)	
Ahaz succeeds Jotham in the 17th year of Pekah (2 K. 15:38; 16:1,2)	3387	659	Ahaz	
Isaiah's prophecy, Ephraim broken in 65 years (Is. 7:8)	3387	659		
Interregnum	3390	656		Interregnum
Hoshea slew Pekah, becoming king in 12th year of Ahaz (2 K. 16:20;18:1,2)	3398	648		Hoshea
Hezekiah's ascends as co-Rex with Ahaz (2 k. 16:20; 18:1,2)	3401	645	Hezekiah	
Death of Ahaz, Isaiah prophecies against Philistines (Isaiah 14:28)	3402	644		
Hezekiah as sole King	3403	643		
Shalmaneser besieges Samaria (2 K. 18:9)	3404	642		
Samaria taken. End of the Kingdom of Israel (2 K. 18:10)	**3406**	**640**		
Events of the 14th year of Hezekiah:	3415	631		
1. Judah invaded by Assyrians under Sennacherib (2 K. 18:13)	3415	631		
2. Jerusalem besieged but overthrown by the angel of the Lord (18:17-19:36)	3415	631		
3. Hezekiah's illness and recovery	3415	631		
4. Visit of Merodach Baladan, king of Babylon (2 K. 20:1-20)	3415	631		
5. Sargon sent Tartan to Ashdod and took it (Is. 20;1; 2 K. 18:17)	3415	631		
6. God adds 15 years to the life of Hezekiah	3415	631		
Manasseh succeeds Hezekiah (2 K. 20;21) after reigning 29 years (2 co-rex)	3430	616	Manasseh	

Explanatory Notes: AN. HOM. = ANNO HOMINIS = The year of the Era of Man, reckoning from the year of the Creation of Adam onward. B.C. = The year of the Era before Christ.

Event	A.H.	B.C.	Judah	Israel
Ephraim broken (Ezra 4:2) fulfilling Isaiah 7:8 by Esar-haddon	3452	594		
Manasseh reigned 55 years succeeded by his son Amon (2 K. 21:1,18)	3485	561	Amon	
Amon reigned 2 years and was slain, succeeded by Josiah (2 K. 21:23-26)	3487	559	Josiah	
Josiah (at 16) "began to seek after the *God of David*" (2 Chr. 34:3)	3495	551		
Josiah purges Judah and Jerusalem by destroying idol-worship	3498	548		
Jeremiah (13th year of Josiah until 4th of Zedekiah) prophesied (Jer. 1:2;25:3)	3499	547		
Purification of Judah and Jerusalem (6 years)	3504	542		
Josiah's (18th): Temple repaired, Book of the law found (2 Chr. 34:8-21)	3505	541		
Josiah's (18th): greatest passover observed since Samuel (2 Chr. 35:18,19)	3505	541		
Josiah killed in battle with Pharaoah Necho, king of Egypt (2 Chr. 36:1)	3517	529		
Jehoahaz reigns 3 months but was carried captive to Egypt	3517	529	Jehoahaz	
Eliakim (Jehoiakim) put on throne by Pharoah Necho (2 Chr. 36:2-4)	3517	529	Jehoiakim	
Jehoiakim's 3rd year Nebudchadnezzar reign as co-Rex (Daniel 1:1)	**3520**	**526**		
1. This was the starting point of the 70 years of the Babylonian Captivity	**3520**	**526**		
2. Daniel and his three companions taken captive to Babylon	3520	526		
3. "Serving the king of Babylon 70 years" prophecy starts (Jer.25:11,12; Dan. 9:2)	3520	526		
Nebuchadnezzar reigned as sole king 4th year of Jehoiakim (Jer. 25:1-3)	3521	525		
1. All nations to serve the king of Babylon 70 years (Jer. 25:11-12)	3521	525		
2. Establishes the date to the overthrow of Babylon by Darius and Cyrus	3521	525		
3. Other prophecies: Jer. 25:1-38; 27:6,7; 36:1,2; 45:1-5; 46:2	3521	525		
Daniel interpreted Nebuchadnezzar's dream of **Great Image** (5th year)	3522	524		
1. Jehoiakim rebelled gainst Nebuchadnezzar (2 Kings 24:1)	3522	524		
2. Jehoiakim cut the Role of the Book with a pen knife & burned it (Jer. 36:22,23)	3522	524		
Nebuchadnezzar took 3023 Jews captive (Jer. 52:28)	3527	519		
Jehoiakim died. Succeeded by Jehoiachin in Nebuchadnezzar's 8th year	3528	518	Jehoiachin	
Jehoiachin reigned 3 months	3528	518	(Jeconiah-Coniah)	
1. Nebuchadnezzar besieged Jerusalem	3528	518		
2. Took Jehoiachin with others captive to Babylon	3528	518		
3. Removed treasures from the Temple (2 kings 24:8-16)	3528	518		
4. Ezekiel was also carried away with Jehoiachin (Ezekiel 1:2; 40:1)	3528	518		

Explanatory Notes: AN. HOM. = ANNO HOMINIS = The year of the Era of Man, reckoning from the year of the Creation of Adam onward.
B.C. = The year of the Era before Christ.

Event	A.H.	B.C.	Judah	Israel
5. Mordecai was also carried away in that captivity (Esth. 2;5,6)	3528	518		
Mattaniah (Zedekiah) was made king in Jehoiachin's stead (2 K. 24:17)	3529	517	Zedekiah	
Ezekiel begins prophecy in 5th year of Jehoiachin's captivity (Ezek. 1:2)	3532	514		
Hannaniah dies due his false prophecy (Jer 28:1-17)	3532	514		
Ezekiel's vision of departure of the **Glory of God** from Temple (Ezek. 8:1)	3533	513		
God refuses to be inquired of (Ezek 20:1-3)	3534	512		
Nebuchadnezzar besieges Jerusalem (2 K. 25:1; Jer.39:1; 52:4)	3537	509		
1. Jeremiah buys his uncle's field in midst of the seige of Jerusalem	3538	508		
2. Jeremiah imprisoned by Zedekiah (Jeremiah 32:1-13)	3538	508		
3. End of Jeremiah's prophecies (Ezekiel's 40 years--Ezekiel 4:5,6)	3538	508		
4. Ezekiel prophesies the same year against Tyre (26:1), Pharoah (30:21); and Egypt (31:1)	3538	508		
Famine prevailed in Jerusalem, city broken up (2 Kings 25:1-4; Jer. 39:2)	3539	507		
1. Same year Nebuzar-adan burnt Temple and broke down walls	3539	507		
2. Jerusalem carried away captive (Jer. 1:3).	3539	507		
3. One comes to Ezekiel and tells him "the city is smitten" (Ezek. 33:21)	3539	507		
4. Ezekiel's lamentation for Pharoah and Egypt (Ezek. 32:1; 32:17)	3539	507		
End of the Kingdom ofJudah in 11th year of Zedekiah (2 K. 24:18)	**3539**	**507**		
Zedekiah carried into Babylonian Captivity	3539	507		
Ezekiel's vision of the new land, city, and temple (Ezekile 40:1)	3552	494		
Jehoiachin set free from prison by Evil Merodach (2 K. 25:27; Jer. 52:31)	3564	482		
Daniel's vision of the **Four Beasts** given/1st year of Belchazzar (Dan. 7:1)	3584	462		
Daniel's vision of the **Ram and He-goat** given (Dan. 8:1)	3586	460		
The overthrow of the kingdom of Babylon	3587	459		
1. The city of Babylon was taken by **Cyrus** (Dan. 5:26-31; Isa. 45:1-4)	3587	459		
2. **Darius** and **Cyrus** rule jointly	3587	459		
3. The vision of the **Seventy Weeks** given to Daniel (Dan. 9:1)	***3587***	***459***		
Cyrus becomes sole king	**3589**	**457**		
1. Cyrus issues proclamaion in his 1st year releasing the captive Jews	**3589**	**457**		
2. Gave them permission to "go up and build the house" (Ezra 1:1-4)	**3589**	**457**		

Explanatory Notes: AN. HOM. = ANNO HOMINIS = The year of the Era of Man, reckoning from the year of the Creation of Adam onward.
B.C. = The year of the Era before Christ.

Event	A.H.	B.C.	Judah	Israel
3. This marks the end of the 70 years "determined" (Daniel 9:24)	**3589**	**457**		
The people began the work of the house of the Lord in Jerusalem (Ezra 3:1-8)	3590	456		
Daniel's Final Great Vision (Dan. 10-11)	**3591**	**455**		
1. Daniel was informed that 3 kings of Persia would arise after Cyrus	3591	455		
2. The fourth king of Persia should be far richer than they all (Dan. 11:2)	3591	455		
3. The fourth king was very wealthy king Xerxes who stirred up all against Greece	3591	455		
4. The "mighty king" who succeeded him was Alexander the Great	3591	455		
5. Alexander's kingdom was divided toward the four winds of heaven	3591	455		
6. This vision was in the 3rd year of Cyrus	3591	455		
Daniel's 70 Week Prophecy (Daniel 9)				
1. From the decree of Cyrus there were to be 69 weeks unto Messiah	**3589**	**457**		
2. The "seven weeks" (49 years) are the measure of the "troublous times"				
3. The street and wall were built in "troublous times" under Ezra and Nehemiah				
4. This bring us (inclusive of the year the decree was issued) to the year = 3637	**3637**	**409**		
5. 1st year of Cyrus "unto Christ", to His baptism is 483 years minus 30 to his birth	**4041**	**5**		
6. Add 30 years to his baptism (15 year of Tiberius Caesar) = 4071	**4071**	AD 26		
7. Add 3 1/2 years to His Crucifixion, Resurrection. Ascension = 4075	**4075**	AD 30		

Explanatory Notes: AN. HOM. = ANNO HOMINIS = The year of the Era of Man, reckoning from the year of the Creation of Adam onward. B.C. = The year of the Era before Christ.

Philip Mauro gives further important reasoning in considering the beginning of the Christian era:

> The Christian Era should properly begin with the year Christ was born; and in devising it, the intention was to have it begin with that year. By the "Christian Era" is meant the system upon which calendars are constructed, and by which historical events are now dated in practically all the civilized world. But the originator of the system made a miscalculation as to the year (in the calendar then in use) in which Christ was born, as the result of which the year A.D. 1 was fixed four years too late. In other words, the Lord Jesus was four years old in the year A.D. 1. The mistake came about in this way: The Christian Era (i.e. the scheme of date beginning A. D. 1) was not devised until A.D. 532. Its inventor, or contriver, was a monk named Dionysius Exiguus. At that time the system of dates in common use began from the era of the emperor Diocletian, A.D. 284. Exiguus was not willing to connect his system of dates with the name of that infamous tyrant and persecutor. So he conceived the idea of connecting his system with, and dating all its events from, the Incarnation of Jesus Christ. His reason for wishing to do this was, as he wrote to Bishop Petronius, 'to the end that the commencement of our hope might be better known to us, and that the cause of man's restoration, namely, our Redeemer's passion, might appear with clearer evidence.' For the carrying out of this excellent plan, it was necessary to fix the date of the Incarnation in the terms of the chronological systems then in vogue. The Romans dated the beginning of their history from the supposed date of the founding of the city (*ab urbe condita* or A.U.C as usually abbreviated). Dionysius Exiguus calculated that the year of our Lord's birth was A.U.C. 753. He made his equivalence of dates from Luke 3:1, "Now in the fifteenth year of the reign of Tiberius Caesar" etc., at which time Christ was 30 years of age according to Luke 3:23. But it was ascertained later that a mistake of four years had been made; for it clearly appears by Matthew 2 that Christ was born before the death of Herod, who died in 749 A.U.C. Tiberius succeeded Augustus, Aug. 19, A.U.C. 767. Hence his 15th year would be A.U.C. 779; and from those facts Dionysius was right in his calculation. But it was discovered in later years that Tiberius began to reign as colleague with Augustus four years before the latter died. Hence the 15th year mentioned by Luke was four years earlier than was supposed by Dionysius, and consequently the birth of Christ was that many years earlier than the date selected by Exiguus, which date has been followed ever since. This must be allowed for in any computation of dates which involves events happening before Christ. We have now found, according to our reckoning, that Christ was born An. Hom. 4041. Therefore, His crucifixion, when He was in His 34th year, would be 4041+34=4075. This is equivalent to 30 A.D.; and to get the true measure of years of any event in our era from the Incarnation it is necessary to add four years to its accepted date. To get the corresponding date in terms of B.C. for any event of Old Testament history, it is only necessary to deduct the years An. Hom. from 4046. For the birth of Christ being 4041 An. Hom. and the Christian era four years later, then B.C. 1 would be equivalent to 4045 which is 4046 - 1.[2]

According to Martin Anstey:

> Ptolemy's Canon is based on the conjectural Greek Chronology of Eratosthenes, the Father of Chronology. The Chronology of Eratosthenes is based, not upon historical data, testimony, evidence or proof, but upon his subjective estimate of the probable length of the reigns, generations and successions of Kings, Ephors and Priestesses in early Greek history. In any case it is only an approximate and an uncertain estimate.[3]

The following chart is a comprehensive listing of the kings and prophets of the kingdoms of Judah and Israel unto their conclusion. The next chart, "The Prophetic Books," gives Bible references concerning the Babylonian Captivity (AH 3520–AH 3589).

The Kings and Prophets of Judah and Israel

Saul	3023 - 3063 AH	1023 - 983 BC	40 Years
David	3063 - 3103 AH	983 - 943 BC	40 Years
Solomon	3103 - 3143 AH	943 - 903 BC	40 Years

Kings of Judah	Beginning of Reign AH BC	Years	Prophets	Kings of Israel	Beginning of Reign AH BC	Years	Prophets
Rehoboam	3143 903	17	Shemaiah	Jeroboam	3143 903	22	Ahijah
Abijam	3160 886	3					
Asa	3163 884	41	Azariah	Nadab	3164 882	1	
			Hanani	Baasha	3165 881	23	Jehu
Jehoshaphat	3204 842	25	Jehaziel	Elah	3188 858	1	
			Eliezer	Omri	3189 857	7 days	
Jehoram	3229 817	3		Tibni	3189 857	11 + 1	Elijah
Ahaziah	3232 814	1		Zimri	3189 857	20 + 2	Elijah
Athaliah	3233 813	6		Ahab	3200 846		Micaiah
Joash	3239 807	40	Joel	Ahaziah	3220 826	1	Elijah
Amaziah	3279 767	29	Joel	Jehoram	3221 825	12	Elisha
Interregnum	3308 738	11	Joel	Jehu	3233 815	28	Elisha
Uzziah	3319 727	52	Isaiah	Jehoahaz	3261 785	17	Elisha
Jotham	3371 675	16	Isaiah/Micah	Jehoash	3278 768	15 + 1	Elisha
Ahaz	3387 659	16	Isaiah	Jeroboam II	3293 753	41	Jonah
			Micah	Interregnum	3334 712	22	Amos
Hezekiah	3403 643	27 + 2	Isaiah				Hosea
		2 co-rex	Micah	Zechariah	3356 690	6 mo.	Hosea
Manasseh	3430 616	55	Nahum	Shallum	3357 689	1 mo.	Hosea
Amon	3485 561	2	Nahum	Menahem	3358 688	10	Hosea
Josiah	3487 559	30	Nahum	Pekahiah	3368 678	2	Hosea
			Zephaniah	Pekah	3370 676	20	Hosea
			Habakkuk	Interregnum	3390 656	8	Micah
			Jeremiah	Hoshea	3398 648	8	Hosea
			Huldah	Fall of Samaria	3406 640		Micah
Jehoahaz	3517 529	3 mo.	Habakkuk	End of the Kingdom of Israel			
			Jeremiah				
Jehoiakim	3517 529	11	Habakkuk				
Babylonian Captivity	3520 526		Jeremiah				
3rd year of Jehoiakim			Daniel				
Jehoiachin	3528 518	3 mo.	Jeremiah				
			Daniel				
Zedekiah	3529 517	10	Jeremiah				
11th and last year of Zedekiah	3539 507		Daniel	End of Kingdom of Judah			

Note: Dates taken from "Romance of Bible Chronology" by Martin Anstey and "Wonders of Bible Chronology by Philip Mauro.

A.H. = Anno Hominis = The year of the era of man, reckoning from the year of the creation of Adam onward.

The Prophetic Books

In the first year of Darius the son of Ahasuerus , of the seed of the Medes, which was made king over the realm of the Chaldeans; In the first year of his *reign I Daniel understood by books the number of the years, whereof the word of the LORD came to Jeremiah the prophet, that he would accomplish seventy years in the desolations of Jerusalem.* And I set my face unto the Lord God, to seek by prayer and supplications, with fasting, and sackcloth, and ashes: And I prayed unto the LORD my God, and made my confession. . . **Daniel 9:1-4a, Emphasis Added**

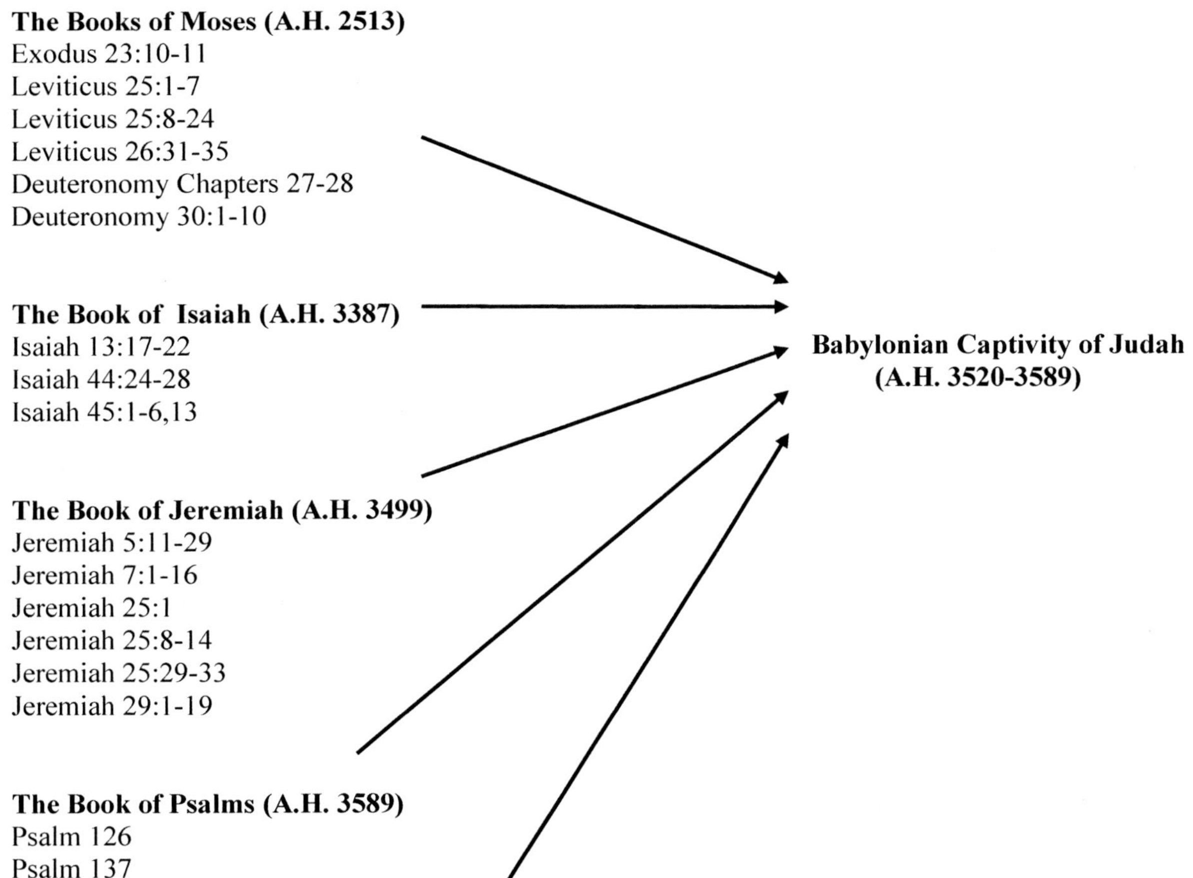

The Book of Kings and Chronicles (A.H. 3119)
1 Kings 8:22-53
2 Chronicles 36:15-21 (A.H. 3589)

DANIEL'S SEVENTY WEEKS PROPHECY

The word *week* is a Hebrew expression which means seven. The word *determined* means divided, decreed, or marked out. Gabriel said to Daniel, "Seventy sevens are decreed upon thy people and upon thy holy city" (Dan. 9:24). Most expositors understand that the "weeks" referred to here are literally "weeks of years." The Hebrews understood the concept of the "weeks of the Lord," and the idea of scripture shows that God indeed was shadowing forth the "redemptive week" in the patterns of the sevens in Israel.

The seventy weeks of Daniel's prophecy involve the "weeks of years," or 490 years. Daniel had studied the prophetic word of Jeremiah and prophesied that the Babylonian captivity would be for seventy (70) years. "For thus saith the LORD, That *after seventy years be accomplished* at Babylon I will visit you, and perform my good word toward you, in causing you to return to this place" (Jer. 29:10, emphasis added).

The reason for this time period was because there was no king of Israel or Judah that had decreed the land must rest every seventh year as God had prophetically commanded through Moses in Leviticus. It was the responsibility of the kings to assure that the land enjoyed the sabbath rests.

> And I will make your cities waste, and bring your sanctuaries unto desolation, and I will not smell the savour of your sweet odours. And I will bring the land into desolation: and your enemies which dwell therein shall be astonished at it. And I will scatter you among the heathen, and will draw out a sword after you: and your land shall be desolate, and your cities waste. *Then shall the land enjoy her sabbaths, as long as it lieth desolate, and ye be in your enemies' land; even then shall the land rest, and enjoy her sabbaths. As long as it lieth desolate it shall rest; because it did not rest in your sabbaths, when ye dwelt upon it.*
>
> —LEVITICUS 26:31–35

Seventy weeks or 490 years were to be decreed or divided throughout Israel's history to bring about the purposes of God.

> Seventy weeks [of years, or 490 years] are decreed upon your people and upon your holy city [Jerusalem], to finish and put an end to transgression, to seal up and make full the measure of sin, to purge away and make expiation and reconciliation for sin, to bring in everlasting righteousness (permanent moral and spiritual rectitude in every area and relation) to seal up vision and prophecy and prophet, and to anoint a Holy of Holies. Know therefore and understand that from the going forth of the commandment to restore and to build Jerusalem until [the coming of] the Anointed One, a Prince, shall be seven weeks [of years] and sixty-two weeks [of years]; it shall be built again with [city] square and moat, but in troublous times.
>
> —DANIEL 9:24–25, AMP

Decree of Cyrus to Messiah the Prince

*"**from** the going forth of the commandment to restore and to build Jerusalem* ***unto*** the Messiah the Prince" Daniel 9:25

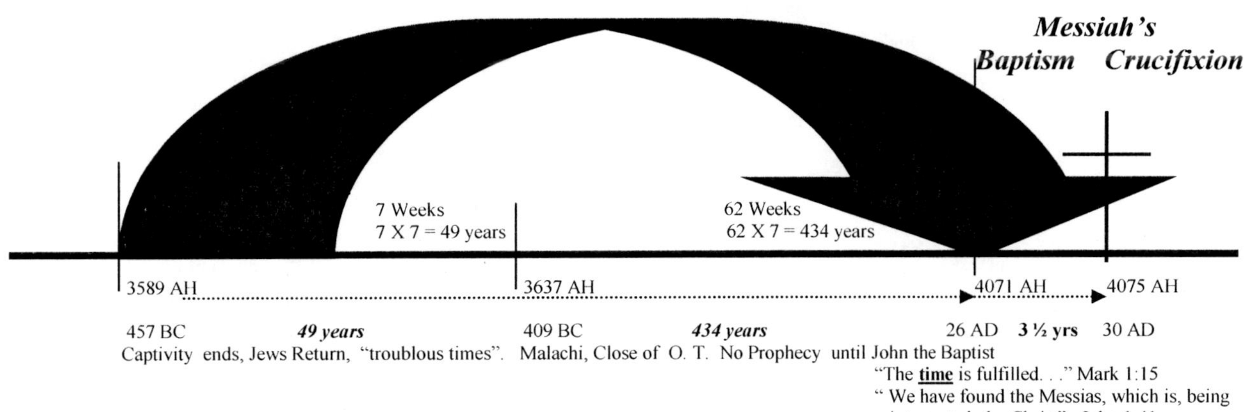

Strong's Exhaustive Concordance of the Bible tells us:

> 2540 // *kairov* // *kairos* // *kahee-ros'* // of uncertain affinity; TDNT - 3:455,389; n m AV - time 64, season 13, opportunity 2, due time 2, always + 1722 + 3956 2, not tr 1, misc 3; 87 1) due measure 2) a measure of time, a larger or smaller portion of time, hence: 2a) a fixed and definite time, the time when things are brought to crisis, the decisive epoch waited for 2b) opportune or seasonable time 2c) the right time 2d) a limited period of time 2e) to what time brings, the state of the times, the things and events of time.[4]

Frank Damazio compares the word *kairos* with *chronos*:

> There are two words in the New Testament for time: *chronos* and *kairos*. *Chronos,* where we get our English word chronology, simply designates a period or space of time. It is close in meaning to the rather scientific way in which westerners speak of time. It is the succession of time, a ration of seasons. *Chronos* expresses the duration of a period, but *kairos* stresses time as being marked by certain features. *Kairos* speaks of a moment of opportunity marked by hearing God's voice afresh and anew. It highlights the significance of that brief or extended moment that *chronos* time brings. Kairos characterizes the content and the quality of the time. It is a moment made significant by a divine encounter with God. The due measure, proportion, or fixed definite period or season may become an opportune or appointed season, based on our seeking God. A *kairos* time is a time where we see prophecy fulfilled, a time when God's purposes are extended.[5]

Consider the *sentence diagram* on the next page of Daniel 9:24–27 to better know and understand the prophecy that Gabriel gave to Daniel:

SENTENCE DIAGRAM OF DANIEL 9:24–27

V. 24 Seventy **weeks** **<u>are determined</u>**
upon thy people
and upon thy holy city
to finish the transgression
to make an end of sins
to make reconciliation for iniquity
to bring in everlasting righteousness
to seal up vision and prophecy
and to anoint the most holy

v.25 **<u>Know</u>** therefore and **<u>understand</u>** *that*
from <u>the going forth of the commandment</u> **(Decree of Cyrus in A.H. 3589)**
to restore **(B.C. 457)**
and to build
Jerusalem
unto
Messiah the Prince **<u>shall be</u>** **(The Lord Jesus Christ A.H. 4071)**
seven weeks (49 years) **(26 A.D.)**
and
threescore and two weeks (434 years)
the **street** **<u>shall be built</u>** again
and the wall
even in troublous times **(A.H. 3589-3637)**

v.26 and
<u>after</u> threescore and two weeks (**<u>after</u>** 434 years)
<u>shall</u> **Messiah** **<u>be cut off</u>** **(The Lord Jesus Christ A.H. 4075)**
but not for himself **(30 A.D.)**
and
the **people** ....**<u>shall destroy</u>**
of the prince the city
that shall come and the sanctuary
and the **end** thereof **<u>shall be</u>**
with a flood
and unto the end of the war
desolations **<u>are determined</u>** **(70 A.D. Romans destroyed Jerusalem)**
<u>and</u>

v.27 **he** **<u>shall confirm</u>** the covenant **(The Lord Jesus Christ A.H. 4071-4075)**
with the many **(Abrahamic Covenant confirmed 26 A.D.- 30 A.D.)**
for one week

[The antecedent for "he" IS NOT "THE *<u>NEAREST</u>* PREVIOUS NOUN", BUT "THE PREVIOUS NOUN <u>IN THE SUBJECTIVE CASE</u>" which is <u>Messiah</u>. Edward Pusey writes: "<u>the prince</u> had not been <u>the subject</u> of any former sentence"]

and
in the midst of the week
he **<u>shall cause to cease</u>** the sacrifice **(The Lord Jesus Christ A.H. 4075)**
and oblation and **(30 A.D.)**
for the overspreading of abominations
he **<u>shall make</u>** it **<u>desolate</u>** **(The Lord Jesus Christ 70 A.D.)**
even until the consummation… and **(Church Age unto the End)**
that determined **<u>shall be poured</u>** upon the desolate. **(Desolator = Antichrist-End of Age)**

A Matter of Grammar

The subjective case: A personal pronoun should be in the *subjective case* (form) if the pronoun functions as a *subject* or *subject complement.* A *subject pronoun* usually comes before the verb; a subject complement pronoun follows a linking verb. Pronouns must match the *number and gender* of the noun they stand for and *be in a case* (form) *that matches its function.* The *noun* that a pronoun refers to is called the *antecedent* of the pronoun.

> An antecedent is the noun, noun phrase, or noun clause that a pronoun refers to in a sentence. It's normally found in a sentence before a pronoun, but it can sometimes also come after that pronoun. In any case, the grammar rule is that any pronoun that refers to this antecedent must agree with it in person (whether first, second, or third person), case (whether nominative or subjective, objective, or possessive), and number (whether singular or plural).[6]

Nearest Noun

> Till another king arose who did not know Joseph. This [Gr. *houtos*] man dealt treacherously with our people, and oppressed our forefathers, making them expose their babies, so that they might not live.
>
> —Acts 7:18–19, NKJV

It is clear in this example that "this" [*houtos*] cannot refer to Joseph, although Joseph is the nearest noun. It refers to the other king, the first one, in the verse, although that evil king is not the nearest noun.

If it is true that pronouns *always* refer to the nearest noun, the result would be serious theological problems. An example is found in Acts 4:10–11: "Let it be known to you all, and to all the people of Israel, that by the name of Jesus Christ of Nazareth, whom you crucified, whom God raised from the dead, by Him this man stands here before you whole. *This* [*houtos*] is the '*stone which was rejected by you builders, which has become the chief cornerstone*'" (NKJV, emphasis added). If "This" in the last sentence refers to the noun or to the nearest pronoun, then the man that was healed is really the stone rejected by the manufacturers that has become head of the corner, that is to say, the Messiah. Of course this conclusion is not true.

It seems to be only a matter of the understanding of English grammar that anyone can decisively determine just who the "he" of verse 27 is in Daniel 9. Verse 26 speaks of (1) Messiah (singular) and (2) the people (plural) of the prince. The "he" of verse 27 is not plural, so it cannot be speaking of the "people of the prince." "Of the prince" is a prepositional phrase of which the "prince" is the object. The *antecedent* of the pronoun "he" in verse 27 cannot not be the "prince" for it *is the object of the prepositional phrase* which acts as an adjective describing the "people."

Which Covenant, Confirmed by Whom?

Stephen Amy has the following comments on the subject:

> Some reject the Messiah as the antecedent of "he" because they are not certain that Jesus made or confirmed any covenants. However, the little horn and beast could be rejected on the same basis since only this verse is used to hypothesize that the little horn or beast will make a covenant. In fact,

> when Jesus was baptized and began to proclaim that the kingdom was at hand, he was causing to be realized a promised, prophesied and covenanted event (cf. Is. 11:1–5, 9:6, 52:13, 53:1–12, Jer. 23:5, Zech. 11:10–12).[7]

> And I took my staff, even Beauty, and cut it asunder, that I might break my covenant which I had made with all the people. And it was broken in that day: and so the poor of the flock that waited upon me knew that it was the word of the Lord. And I said unto them, If ye think good, give me my price; and if not, forbear. So they weighed for my price thirty pieces of silver. And the Lord said unto me, Cast it unto the potter: a goodly price that I was prised at of them. And I took the thirty pieces of silver, and cast them to the potter in the house of the Lord.
>
> —Zechariah 11:10–13

Amy continues:

> In the above Zechariah reference (11:10–13) there is no doubt that the Messiah in His first advent is in view, and that the Messiah "breaks" a covenant because of the behavior of the "sheep." In that passage the Messiah is betrayed for thirty pieces of silver and killed (11:13). The "covenant" of Daniel 9:27 is not some new covenant referred to here for the first time, but "*the* covenant" (Hebrew). The fact that *the* covenant is "confirmed" is further notice that this is a covenant spoken of elsewhere in Scriptures. The proposal, that the covenant mentioned here *is a covenant made with Israel by the antichrist*, is *a hypothesis, assumption, or guess*, and *is not presented or supported in any other scriptures*.[8]

> The Scripture, foreseeing that God would justify the Gentiles by faith, preached the gospel beforehand to Abraham, *saying*, "All the nations will be blessed in you." So then those who are of faith are blessed with Abraham, the believer. For as many as are of the works of the Law are under a curse; for it is written, "Cursed is everyone who does not abide by all things written in the book of the law, to perform them." Now that no one is justified by the Law before God is evident; for, "The righteous man shall live by faith." However, the Law is not of faith; on the contrary, "He who practices them shall live by them." Christ redeemed us from the curse of the Law, having become a curse for us—for it is written, "Cursed is everyone who hangs on a tree"—in order that in Christ Jesus the blessing of Abraham might come to the Gentiles, so that we would receive the promise of the Spirit through faith. Brethren, I speak in terms of human relations: even though it is *only* a man's covenant, yet when it has been ratified, no one sets it aside or adds conditions to it. Now the promises were spoken to Abraham and to his seed. He does not say, "And to seeds," as *referring* to many, but *rather* to one, "And to your seed," that is, Christ. What I am saying is this: the Law, which came four hundred and thirty years later, does not invalidate a covenant previously ratified by God, so as to nullify the promise.
>
> —Galatians 3:8–17, nas

> And I will bless those who bless you, And the one who curses you I will curse. And in you all the families of the earth will be blessed.
>
> —Genesis 12:3, nas

The following chart exemplifies the period from the decree of Cyrus to the destruction of Jerusalem by the Roman armies in AD 70.

Decree of Cyrus to the Destruction of Jerusalem AD 70

". . .from the going forth of the commandment to restore and to build Jerusalem unto Messiah the Prince shall be seven weeks and threescore and two weeks" Daniel 9:25

"And **AFTER** threescore and two weeks shall Messiah be cut off, but not for Himself:

And the people of the prince that shall come shall destroy the city and the sanctuary; and the end shall be with a flood, and unto the end of the war desolations are determined." Daniel 9:26

70 Week Prophecy
Daniel

"The street shall be built again, and the wall even in troublous times"

Close of O.T.
Malachi

No Prophecy

Messiah
Manifest

"We have found Messias"
Baptism
of Jesus by John the Baptist

Siege and destruction of Jerusalem by Roman soldiers led by prince Titus in 70 AD.

Jesus Christ Confirms Covenant
Daniel 9:27 and Romans 15:7

3589 AH 457 BC	**7 Weeks** **(49 years)**	3637 AH 409 BC	**62 Weeks** **(434 years)**	**4071 AH** **26 AD**	**½ Week** **(3 ½ yrs)**	**4075 AH** **30 AD**	**40 years**	**4115 AH** **70 AD**
		49 Years		**483 Years**		**486 ½ Years**		

[1st Half of Daniel's 70th Week]

Ezra, Nehemiah, Haggai, Zechariah, Zerubbabel, Malachi

"and in the midst of the week He shall cause the sacrifice and oblation to cease, and **for the overspreading of abominations** he shall make it desolate, ... even unto **the consummation**"

Church Age unto THE END

"When ye therefore shall see the abomination of desolation, spoken of by Daniel the prophet, stand in the holy place. . .let them which be in Judea flee unto the mountains. . ." Matthew 24:15,16a

O Jerusalem, Jerusalem, thou that killest the prophets, and stonest them which are sent unto thee, how often would I have gathered thy children together, even as a hen gathereth her chickens under her wings, and you would not. Matthew 23 37

Behold, your house is left unto you DESOLATE. Matthew 23:38

Kevin Conner has the following comments on the subject:

THE MATERIAL TEMPLE WAS FINISHED:

1. THE FATHER rent the veil of the temple before the High Priest in connection with the sacrifice of His only begotten Son, who caused all sacrifice and oblation to cease. It was an act of God declaring that He no longer accepted the blood of animals, which He had once ordained now that that He had the TRUE SACRIFICE. Christ's was the sacrifice of all sacrifices! (Matthew 27:1-51). The rending of the veil signifies the end of the Dispensation of the Law Covenant and all that pertained to Mosaic ritualism.

2. THE SON after cleansing the Temple at the beginning and end of His ministry (one half a week, or, 3 ½ years), Christ prophesied that the temple would be destroyed and the Abomination of Desolation would be manifest. He never ever returned to the Temple after that. He saw that it was no longer his FATHER'S HOUSE, but Jewry's house.

3. THE HOLY SPIRIT on the Day of Pentecost, the Holy Spirit by-passed the Temple as Jewry kept the letter and form of the Law concerning the Feast. He went to an upper room where the TRUE Pentecost was kept, and there the TRUE TEMPLE was dedicated – that is, the New Testament Church! If the Father and Son had finished with the Temple, so was the Holy Spirit finished with it. He came to dwell as the Shekinah Glory in the New Covenant Temple, the people of God.

> The greatest desolation is that Jewry has been desolate of Temple, Priest and Sanctuary ever since AD 70, when Prince Titus, the son of the Roman Emperor Vespasian, came to Jerusalem with the Roman armies and besieged it. Jewry was scattered to the four corners of earth. The city, the sanctuary, the land and the people were desolated and have been ever since. This condition is to continue until the Times of the Gentiles are fulfilled. (See Matthew 24:1-2; Daniel 9:26; Isaiah 8:7,8; 28:18; 10:23; 28:22; Psalm 90:5; Deuteronomy 29:49-67 with Leviticus 26).
>
> "And that determined shall be poured upon the desolate" (v. 27). The Marginal reading says, "The Desolator". The details of the consummation are left to the Book of Revelation, the Book of the Time of the End. The final and ultimate abomination that brings desolation is the worship of the Antichrist Beast and the taking of his mark, number and name. All who do so shall suffer eternal damnation. The "pouring out" spoken of here finds fulfillment in Revelation 15-16 in the vials (bowls) of wrath that are "poured out" on a desolate world of Antichrist worshippers. When people reject the "outpoured Holy Spirit" in mercy, then they have no alternative but to suffer the "outpoured wrath" of God in judgment.[9]

The following chart shows the epoch of the seven weeks in Daniel 9—the decree of Cyrus (AH 3589) to the close of the Old Testament (AH 3637) and then on to the Crucifixion (AH 4075).

Epoch of the Seven Weeks in Daniel 9

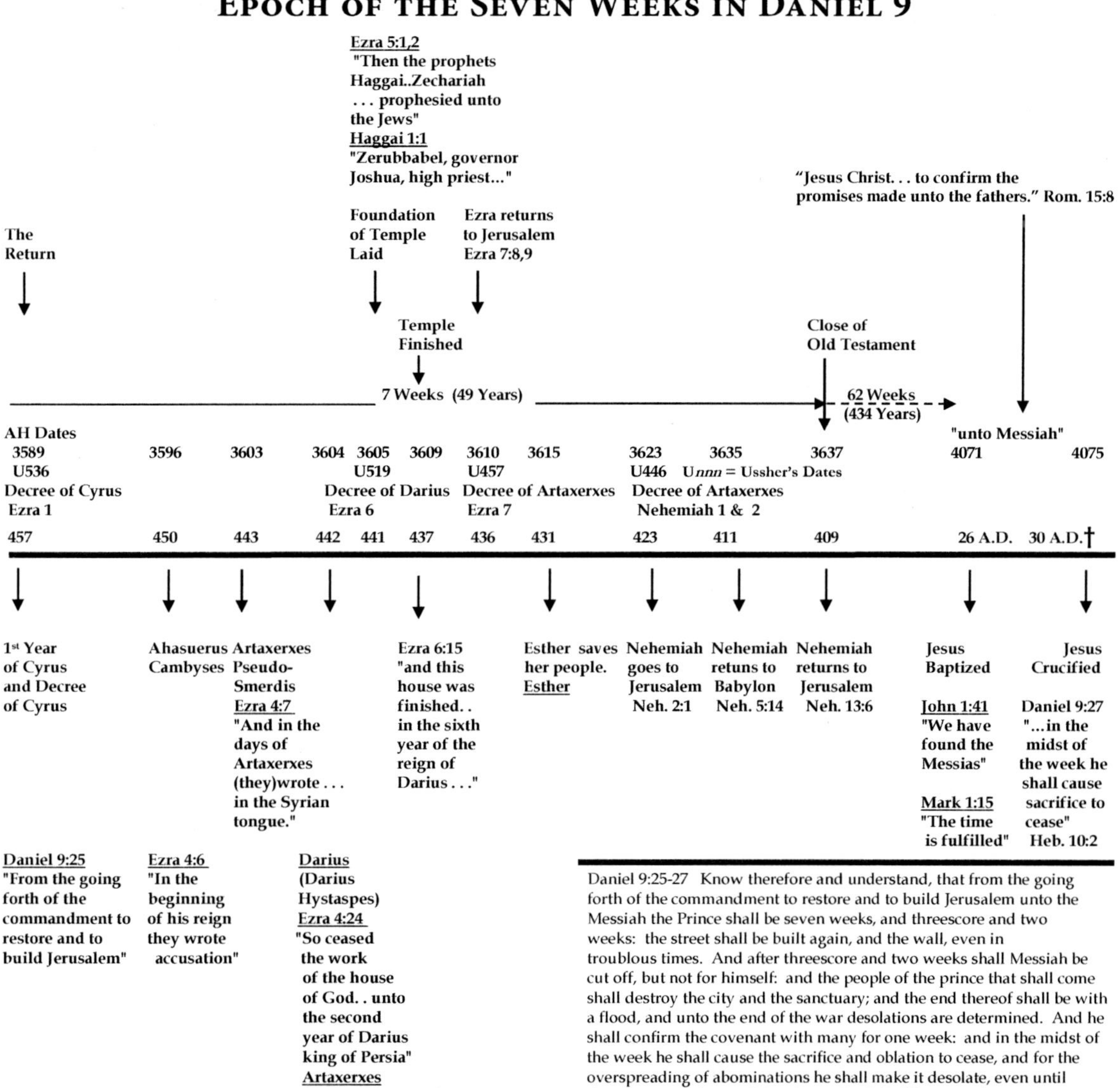

Four Decrees of Four Persian Kings

Some think that Cyrus's decree only had to do with the rebuilding the temple (or house) and not to the building of the city of Jerusalem! They use this scripture as proof:

> Now in the first year of Cyrus king of Persia, that the word of the Lord spoken by the mouth of Jeremiah might be accomplished, the Lord stirred up the spirit of Cyrus king of Persia, that he made a proclamation throughout all his kingdom, and put it also in writing, saying, Thus saith Cyrus king of Persia, All the kingdoms of the earth hath the Lord God of heaven given me; and *he hath charged me to build him an house in Jerusalem,* which is in Judah. Who is there among you of all his people? The Lord his God be with him, and let him go up.
>
> —2 Chronicles 36:22–23, emphasis added

But they seem to be unaware of the prophecies of Isaiah 44:26–28 and Isaiah 45:1, 13, in which Cyrus would perform *all* God's pleasure:

> That confirmeth the word of his servant, and performeth the counsel of his messengers; that saith to Jerusalem, Thou shalt be inhabited; and to the cities of Judah, Ye shall be built, *and* I will raise up the decayed places thereof... That saith of Cyrus, He is my shepherd, and shall perform all my pleasure: even *saying to Jerusalem, Thou shalt be built; and to the temple, Thy foundation shall be laid.*
>
> —ISAIAH 44:26, 28, EMPHASIS ADDED

It is absolutely necessary to be "intellectually honest" with the Scriptures. Reading down a few more verses in Isaiah 45:1–3 and v. 13, the interpreter would see that this is *confirmed again*:

> Thus saith the LORD to his anointed, to *Cyrus*, whose right hand I have holden, to subdue nations before him; and I will loose the loins of kings, to open before him the two leaved gates... I have raised him up in righteousness, and I will direct all his ways: *he shall build my city, and he shall let go my captives*, not for price nor reward, saith the LORD of hosts.
>
> —ISAIAH 45:1, 13, EMPHASIS ADDED

Bible scholars would be wise to stick with Bible dates only. Of course, if they did, they would have to change not only their chronology but also their eschatology. The following charts show four Persian kings' decrees broken down into *Ptolemaic dates* and *Bible Dates*. This way one can *visualize on one page* the various concepts and make an easy yet forthright analysis. Observe that the Bible dates chart uses *only* Bible dates. We start with the *Decree of Cyrus* in AH 3589, which is 457 adjusted BC date, and conclude 483 years later with AH 4071 or AD 26. If you choose to use the Ptolemaic dating system, you would end up having to use the *third decree of Artaxerxes* in order to be able to end with AD 26, which just happens to be *eighty years difference* than the decree of Cyrus. Using the Ptolemaic dates is not valid.

Four Decrees of Four Persian Kings

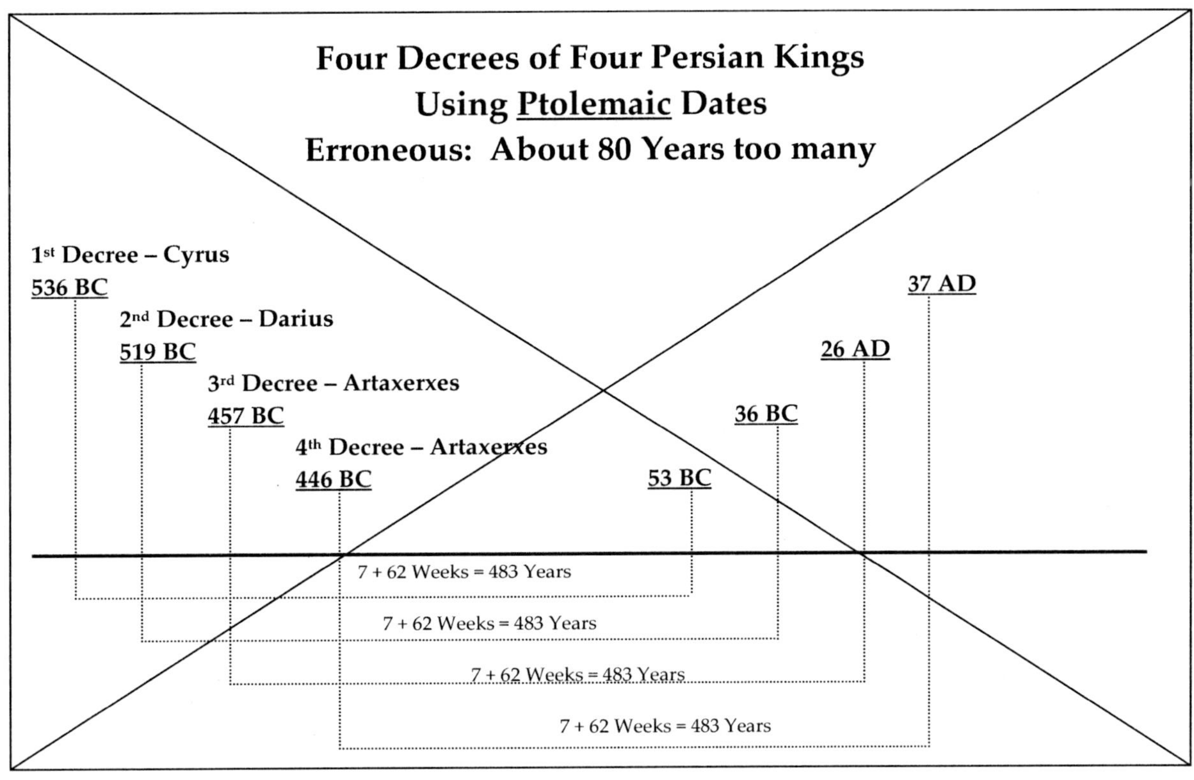

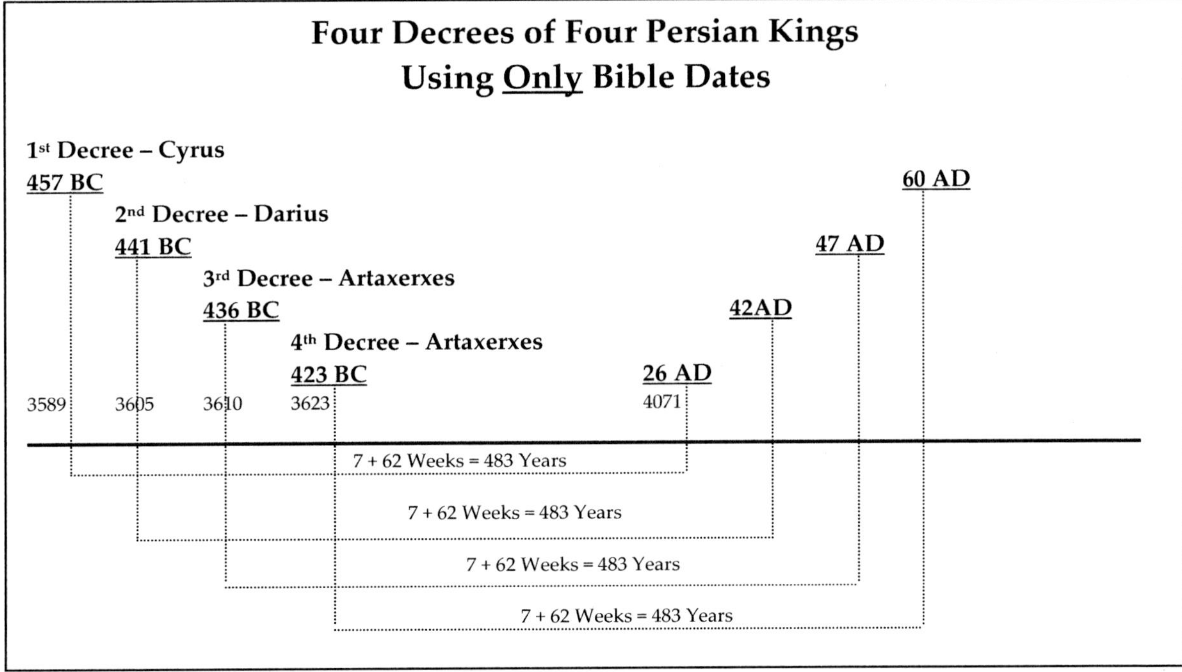

The following table and chart were designed to demonstrate six 490-year periods in Scripture simply by using Bible dates.

490 YEAR PERIODS IN SCRIPTURE TABLE

1st

From the birth of Abraham to the Exodus was actually 505 years, but by deducting the 15 years while Ishmael was Abram's seed, delaying the seed of promise, (Gen 12:4, 16:3 and 21:5) = 490 years. (2008 – 2513 = 505 years minus 15 years = 490 years) the *first* 70 x 7 of years in Scripture.

2nd

From the Abrahamic Covenant when Abraham was 75 years old until the beginning of the period of the Judges = 490 years (2083-2573).

3rd

From the Exodus until the beginning of the judgeship of Samuel = 490 years (2513 – 3003). (Seen in another way, from the beginning of the Law until the beginning of the Prophets).

4th

From the beginning of the period of the Judges until the first year of the reign of King David = 490 years (2573 – 3063).

5th

From the end of the seventh year of King Saul's reign until the beginning of the Babylonian Captivity = 490 years (3030 – 3520). (Leviticus 26:33-45, Jeremiah 25:11,12, Daniel 9:2.)

6th

Daniel's 70-Week Prophecy = 490 years (3589 – 4071) = 483 years + 3 ½ years unto the Crucifixion + 3 ½ years Tribulation (Book of Daniel 9 and 12 with Revelation 10).

The number *seven*, significant of *spiritual perfection* in Scriptures. That significance is amplified when multiplied by 70, in other words (70 X 7). So we dramatically see in Scriptures 490 year epochs which remind us that God is the **Father of all Time** and **Potter of all Ages**?

490 Year Periods in Scripture Chart

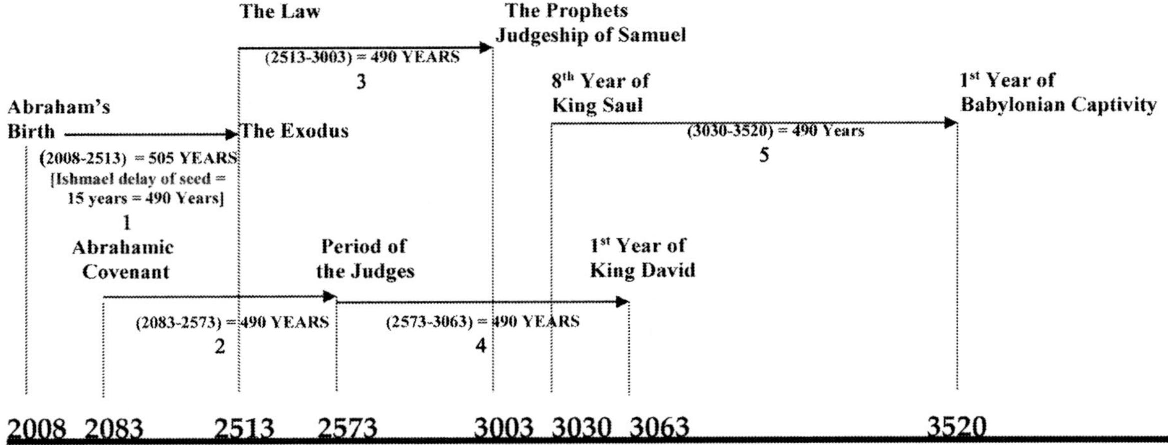

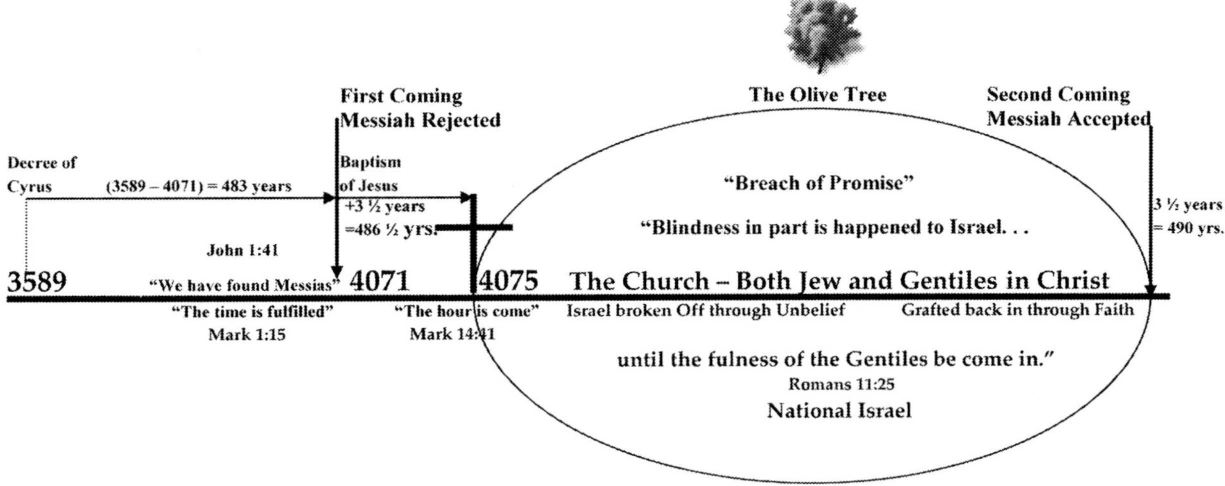

The breaches of promise are caused by unbelief, while breaches of time are caused by the prophet's viewing separated events as one. That which is revealed in Scripture concerning the many breaches of time and promise only further substantiates and illustrates the fact that God both transcends and controls time. The breaches of time are not to be viewed as having caused the time clock of God's eternal purpose to stop running. Man's failure, as illustrated in the breaches of promise, did not alter God's scheduled purposes. Jesus Christ came as the promised Messiah to the chosen nation of Israel, confirming the promises made to the fathers. However, according to the prophecy of Isaiah, the nation as a whole had ears and could not hear, eyes and could not see, and a heart that could not perceive (Isaiah 6:9,10). Through the spiritual blindness of their unbelief they could not see Jesus as their promised Messiah. (Matthew 13:14,15; Acts 28:25-27)[10]

Chapter 8
SEEING DAYS 5 AND 6

First Coming to Second Coming (about 2,000 Years)

Unto him be glory in the church by Christ Jesus throughout all ages, world without end. Amen.
—Ephesians 3:21

With the coming of Messiah (the Lord Jesus Christ) came Light into this world of darkness:

> The people that walked in darkness have seen a great light: they that dwell in the land of the shadow of death, upon them hath the light shined.
>
> —Isaiah 9:2

> In the beginning was the Word, and the Word was with God, and the Word was God. The same was in the beginning with God. All things were made by him; and without him was not any thing made that was made. In him was life; and the life was the light of men. And the light shineth in darkness; and the darkness comprehended it not. There was a man sent from God, whose name was John. The same came for a witness, to bear witness of the Light, that all men through him might believe. He was not that Light, but was sent to bear witness of that Light. That was the true Light, which lighteth every man that cometh into the world.
>
> —John 1:1–9

From the baptism of the Lord Jesus in the river Jordan by John the Baptist unto Christ's crucifixion, Jesus shined forth with the exact representation (mirror image) of His Father:

> God, who at sundry times and in divers manners spake in time past unto the fathers by the prophets, Hath in these last days spoken unto us by his Son, whom he hath appointed heir of all things, by whom also he made the worlds; *Who being the brightness of his glory, and the express image of his person*, and upholding all things by the word of his power, when he had by himself purged our sins, sat down on the right hand of the Majesty on high.
>
> —Hebrews 1:1–3, emphasis added

After His crucifixion, burial, resurrection, and ascension, Jesus told His disciples to wait for the promise of the Father.

> To whom also he shewed himself alive after his passion by many infallible proofs, being seen of them forty days, and speaking of the things pertaining to the kingdom of God: And, being assembled together with them, commanded them that they should not depart from Jerusalem, but *wait for the*

> *promise of the Father*, which, saith he, ye have heard of me. For John truly baptized with water; but ye shall be baptized with the Holy Ghost not many days hence.
>
> —Acts 1:3–5, emphasis added

The church was divinely lit on the Day of Pentecost. After being divinely lit, it was the function of the priests to maintain that light. Today's order of priesthood is a *higher order of priesthood* than the Aaronic priesthood, we are of the order of Melchizedek with Christ as our High Priest, we are "a *royal priesthood* [as kings and priests unto God]...that we should shew forth the praises of him who hath called you out of darkness into his marvelous light" (1 Pet. 2:9, emphasis added).

The early church had turned the then known world upside down with the *light* they revealed through the demonstration of the power of the Holy Spirit.

After believers experience salvation by faith in the Lord Jesus Christ, water baptism, Holy Spirit baptism, and walking in holiness, *the next step was to become ministers of reconciliation* (i.e., drawing those lost into a favorable relationship with God).

> Therefore if any man be in Christ, he is a new creature: old things are passed away; behold, all things are become new. And all things are of God, who hath reconciled us to himself by Jesus Christ, and hath *given to us the ministry of reconciliation*; To wit, that God was in Christ, reconciling the world unto himself, *not imputing their trespasses unto them; and hath committed unto us the word of reconciliation*. Now then we are ambassadors for Christ, as though God did beseech you by us: we pray you in Christ's stead, be ye reconciled to God.
>
> —2 Corinthians 5:17–20, emphasis added

It is the Holy Spirit fire that motivates a believer to be an effective witness for the Lord. It is that baptism of fire that is the spark that ignites the soul of a believer to bear witness of the Lord Jesus Christ. Without the Holy Spirit, the Strengthener (or, One who empowers), believers can do nothing.

> Then I said, I will not make mention of him, nor speak any more in his name. *But his word was in mine heart as a burning fire shut up in my bones, and I was weary with forbearing, and I could not stay.*
>
> —Jeremiah 20:9, emphasis added

> When they therefore were come together, they asked of him, saying, Lord, wilt thou at this time restore again the kingdom to Israel? And he said unto them, It is not for you to know the times or the seasons, which the Father hath put in his own power. But ye shall receive power, after that the Holy Ghost is come upon you: and ye shall be witnesses unto me both in Jerusalem, and in all Judaea, and in Samaria, and unto the uttermost part of the earth.
>
> —Acts 1:6–8

The church *today* is still completely dependent upon the infilling of the Holy Spirit. The Spirit of God, whom Jesus sent, gives us great knowledge about God as well as showing the path that we take.

> But the people that do know their God shall be strong, and do exploits.
>
> —Daniel 11:32b

The early church relied on the power of the Holy Spirit for them to witness effectively unto Jesus throughout the world. It is the Spirit of Christ. We need to be in the presence of Jesus continually for Him to help us. It is the Spirit of holiness that brings "resurrection life."

> And declared to be the Son of God with power, according to the spirit of holiness, by the resurrection from the dead.
>
> —Romans 1:4, emphasis added

The Holy Spirit will give the believer a strong desire to know God and to how to apply the Holy Scriptures.

> As newborn babes, *desire* [greatly desire] *the sincere milk of the word, that ye may grow thereby*: If so be ye have tasted that the Lord is gracious.
>
> —1 Peter 2:2–3, emphasis added

> Whom shall he teach knowledge? and whom shall he make to understand doctrine? them that are weaned from the milk, and drawn from the breasts. For precept must be upon precept, precept upon precept; line upon line, line upon line; here a little, and there a little: *For with stammering lips and another tongue will he speak to this people.*
>
> —Isaiah 28:9–11, emphasis added

One of the means of grace God has given to us is *the assembling of ourselves together.* It is vital as we see the day of His coming drawing near.

> *Not forsaking the assembling of ourselves together,* as the manner of some is; but exhorting one another: and so much the more, as ye see the day approaching.
>
> —Hebrews 10:25, emphasis added

> How is it then, brethren? *when ye come together,* every one of you hath a psalm, hath a doctrine, hath a tongue, hath a revelation, hath an interpretation. *Let all things be done unto edifying.*
>
> —1 Corinthians 14:26, emphasis added

> The sceptre shall not depart from Judah, nor a lawgiver from between his feet, until Shiloh come; and *unto him shall the gathering of the people be.*
>
> —Genesis 49:10, emphasis added

Since the inauguration of the church on the Day of Pentecost, there has been both a *decline* and *restoration* throughout the history of the church. (For an excellent study on this theme, the book *Present Day Truths* by K. R. (Dick) Iverson with Bill Scheidler is highly recommended.)

By the second century AD, the church's light began to dim and it became similar to the dark days of the judges. Pentecostal pioneer Donald Gee once said, "It is surely a serious thing to accuse God of withdrawing the gifts of the Holy Spirit when the church lost them because of their own lukewarmness."

But then God raised up Luther, Calvin, the Wesley brothers, Finney, and others; and little by little the light and truths of the Word of God began to be restored and God's temple became brighter and brighter, for the Lord was preparing His bride in Day 6—the last truth lost was the first to be restored.

As in Creation, the sixth day in which the beasts were created, even so there will be great darkness in these last days. It was on the sixth day that man and woman were also created. Ephesians 4:13 says, "Till we all come to the unity of the faith and the of knowledge of the Son of God, to *a perfect man*, to the measure of the stature of the fullness of Christ" (NKJV, emphasis added).

For that man to be "perfect" (the bride of Christ, the body of Christ, the people of God of all ages), God's call to His people is to "come out of her [Babylon], my people, lest you share in her sins, and lest you receive of her plagues. For her sins have reached to heaven, and God has remembered her iniquities" (Rev, 18:4–5, NKJV). And, of Babylon the great, it is said:

> And *the light of a lamp shall not shine in you anymore.* And the voice of bridgroom and bride shall not be heard in you anymore. For your merchants were the great men of the earth, for by your sorcery all the nations were deceived. And in her was found the blood of prophets and saints, and of all who were slain on the earth.
>
> —REVELATION 18:23–24, NKJV, EMPHASIS ADDED

> And after these things I heard a great voice of much people in heaven saying, Alleluia…and I heard as it were the voice of a great multitude, and as the voice of many waters, and as the voice of mighty thunderings, saying, Alleluia, for the Lord God omnipotent reigneth. Let us be glad and rejoice and give honour to him: for the marriage of the Lamb is come, and his wife hath made herself ready.
>
> —REVELATION 19:1, 6–7

And then is the marriage supper of the Lamb. Kevin Conner comments:

> The Old Covenant Church, Natural Israel, once the disciples accepted Christ Jesus, became members of the New Covenant Church, Spiritual Israel. This church becomes the true Israel of God entitled to the spiritual promises of the Abrahamic Covenant. This Church is taken out of every kindred, every tongue, and every tribe and nation. Whereas the Old Covenant Church was basically one nation, Israel, now the New Covenant Church is from all nations. Abraham was to be the father of many nations, not just the one chosen nation (Genesis 12:2–3; 17:1–8). Abraham was to be the father of all who believe, whether from Israel as a nation or the Gentile nations. Romans 4 shows that Abraham was the father of the Circumcision and the Uncircumcision, that is, believing Jews and believing Gentiles.[1]

> "Blessed is the man to whom the Lord will not impute sin. Cometh this blessedness then upon the circumcision only, or upon the uncircumcision also? for we say that *faith was reckoned to Abraham for righteousness. How was it then reckoned? when he was in circumcision, or in uncircumcision? Not in circumcision, but in uncircumcision.*
>
> —ROMANS 4:8–10, EMPHASIS ADDED

Conner continues:

> Futurists and Dispensationalists charge other Millennial Schools of thought of 'robbing Israel of her inheritance' and 'teaching replacement theology, that the Church replaces Israel.' This is not the case. Israel's true inheritance was 'in Christ' and those of Israel or Judah who accepted Christ continued on in their inheritance in the New Testament Church. The Church does not "replace natural or national Israel.' The New Covenant Church is the continuation of the true and believing Israel of God from

Old Covenant times. However, it is in a higher level of the New Covenant, the Old having been fulfilled and abolished at the Cross. It is the unbelieving Jew or Israelite who actually robs himself when he rejects Christ as his Saviour.[2]

> For he is not a Jew, which is one outwardly; neither is that circumcision, which is outward in the flesh: But he is a Jew, which is one inwardly; and circumcision is that of the heart, in the spirit, and not in the letter; whose praise is not of men, but of God.
>
> —ROMANS 2:28–29

> Therefore it is of faith, that it might be by grace; to the end the promise might be sure to all the seed; not to that only which is of the law, but to that also which is of the faith of Abraham; who is *the father of us all*, (As it is written, I have made thee a father of many nations,) before him whom he believed, even God, who quickeneth the dead, and calleth those things which be not as though they were.
>
> —ROMANS 4:16–17, EMPHASIS ADDED

> Not as though the word of God hath taken none effect. *For they are not all Israel, which are of Israel*: Neither, because they are the seed of Abraham, are they all children: but, In Isaac shall thy seed be called. That is, They which are the children of the flesh, these are not the children of God: but *the children of the promise are counted for the seed.*
>
> —ROMANS 9:6–8, EMPHASIS ADDED

Because of Christ's work of redemption on the cross, the middle wall of partition between the Jew and the Gentile was broken down. *And so of two—Jews and Gentiles—He made one new man*:

> That at that time ye were without Christ, being aliens from the commonwealth of Israel, and strangers from the covenants of promise, having no hope, and without God in the world: But now in Christ Jesus ye who sometimes were far off are made nigh by the blood of Christ. For he is our peace, who hath made both one, and hath broken down the middle wall of partition between us; Having abolished in his flesh the enmity, even the law of commandments contained in ordinances; *for to make in himself of twain one new man*, so making peace; And that he might reconcile both unto God in one body by the cross, having slain the enmity thereby.
>
> —EPHESIANS 2:12–16, EMPHASIS ADDED

> Jesus saith unto them, Did ye never read in the scriptures, The stone which the builders rejected, the same is become the head of the corner: this is the Lord's doing, and it is marvellous in our eyes? Therefore say I unto you, *The kingdom of God shall be taken from you, and given to a nation bringing forth the fruits thereof.* And whosoever shall fall on this stone shall be broken: but on whomsoever it shall fall, it will grind him to powder.
>
> —MATTHEW 21:42–44, EMPHASIS ADDED

The following chart sets forth the timeline of days 5 and 6:

Days 5 and 6

Day 5

Birth of JESUS	"unto Messiah"		Apostolic Church	Persecuted Church	Imperial Church	Medieval Church
4041	**4071**	**4075**	**Early Rain**			
5 B.C.	26 A.D.	30 A.D.	30-100 A.D.	100-313 A.D.	313-476 A.D.	476-
	His Anointing	**Crucifixion Resurrection Ascension Pentecost**				

Day 6

Medieval Church (cont.)	Reformed Church	Modern Church	Pentecost Restored
-1453	1453-1648	1648-1900	1900-Present

Stages of the Church in Days 5 and 6

Apostolic Church (30-100)
- Signs and Wonders
- Ministries (Apostles, Prophets, Evangelists, Pastors, Teachers)
- Death of John

Persecuted Church (100-313)
- Martyrs
- New Testament Church

Imperial Church (313-476)
- Decline
- Edict of Constantine
- Victory of Christianity
- Growing Power of the Roman Catholic Church
- Fall of Rome

Medieval Church (476-1453)
- Pope Gains Power over Kings
- Fall of Constantinople
- Wycliffe Translates First English Bible (1170)

Reformed Church (1453-1648)
- Martin Luther (1517)
- John Calvin (1528)
- John Knox (1547)
- Protestants Won Victory in 30 Years War
- Quakers (1647)

Modern Church (1648-1900)
- Holiness Movement
- John Wesley

Pentecost Restored (Speaking in Tongues in **1900**--Revivals in **1906**)

1. Warnings by Paul

> Take heed therefore unto yourselves, and to all the flock, over the which the Holy Ghost hath made you overseers, to feed the church of God, which he hath purchased with his own blood. For I know this, that *after my departing shall grievous wolves enter in among you, not sparing the flock.* Also of your own selves shall men arise, speaking perverse things, to draw away disciples after them.
>
> —ACTS 20:28–30, EMPHASIS ADDED

> Now the Spirit speaketh expressly, that *in the latter times some shall depart from the faith,* giving heed to seducing spirits, and doctrines of devils; Speaking lies in hypocrisy; having their conscience seared with a hot iron; Forbidding to marry, and commanding to abstain from meats, which God hath created to be received with thanksgiving of them which believe and know the truth. For every creature of God is good, and nothing to be refused, if it be received with thanksgiving.
>
> —1 TIMOTHY 4:1–4, EMPHASIS ADDED

2. Warnings by Peter

> But there were false prophets also among the people, *even as there shall be false teachers among you, who privily shall bring in damnable heresies, even denying the Lord that bought them, and bring upon themselves swift destruction. And many shall follow their pernicious ways; by reason of whom the way of truth shall be evil spoken of.*
>
> —2 PETER 2:1–2, EMPHASIS ADDED

3. Warnings by John

> I wrote unto the church: but Diotrephes, who loveth to have the preeminence among them, receiveth us not. Wherefore, if I come, I will remember his deeds which he doeth, prating against us with malicious words: and not content therewith, neither doth he himself receive the brethren, and forbiddeth them that would, and casteth them out of the church. *Beloved, follow not that which is evil, but that which is good. He that doeth good is of God: but he that doeth evil hath not seen God.*
>
> —3 JOHN 1:9–11, EMPHASIS ADDED

> Notwithstanding I have a few things against thee, *because thou sufferest that woman Jezebel, which calleth herself a prophetess, to teach and to seduce my servants to commit fornication, and to eat things sacrificed unto idols.* And I gave her space to repent of her fornication; and she repented not. Behold, I will cast her into a bed, and them that commit adultery with her into great tribulation, except they repent of their deeds. And I will kill her children with death; and all the churches shall know that I am he which searcheth the reins and hearts: and I will give unto every one of you according to your works.
>
> —REVELATION 2:20–23, EMPHASIS ADDED

4. Warnings by Jude

> For there are *certain men crept in unawares, who were before of old ordained to this condemnation, ungodly men, turning the grace of our God into lasciviousness, and denying the only Lord God, and our Lord Jesus Christ.*
>
> —JUDE 1:4, EMPHASIS ADDED

In their book *Present Day Truths*, Iverson and Scheidler have the following insights for the decline of power in the church:

> One looks at the condition of the Church in the Middle Ages and naturally asks, "How could the people be so blinded to the truth? How could they believe that what they were practicing was true Christianity?" We must remember that in the time between the death of the apostles and the Dark Ages the changes that took place were subtle and gradual. Possibly the chief cause of decline of the Church was its mixture with the things and practices of pagan religions and the world which became progressively manifest. Because of the total commitment and persecution witnessed in the Early Church, believers were forced to cling to the Lord and the communion of the saints. There was no place for the believer in the world. People who became Christians adopted an entirely different life-style from their past life. They were indeed the CALLED OUT ONES.[3]

Stages of the Church in Days Five and Six

- Apostolic Church (30–100)
  - Signs and Wonders
  - Ministries (Apostles, Prophets, Evangelists, Pastors, Teachers)
  - Death of John
- Persecuted Church (100–313)
  - Martyrs
  - New Testament Church
- Imperial Church (313–476)
  - Decline
  - Edict of Constantine
  - Victory of Christianity
  - Growing Power of the Roman Catholic Church
  - Fall of Rome
- Medieval Church (476–1453)
  - Pope Gains Power over Kings
  - Fall of Constantinople
  - Wycliffe Translates First English Bible (1170)
- Reformed Church (1453–1648)
  - Martin Luther (1517)
  - John Calvin (1528)
  - John Knox (1547)
  - Protestants Won Victory in 30 Years War
  - Quakers (1647)
- Modern Church (1648–1900)
  - Holiness Movement

John Wesley

- Pentecost Restored (Speaking in Tongues January 1, 1901, Revivals in 1906)

The following diagram shows how the church declined in power and yet the process of restoration began when men of God spoke out with messages of truth to the people.

Restoration of the Church (from Decline to Power)

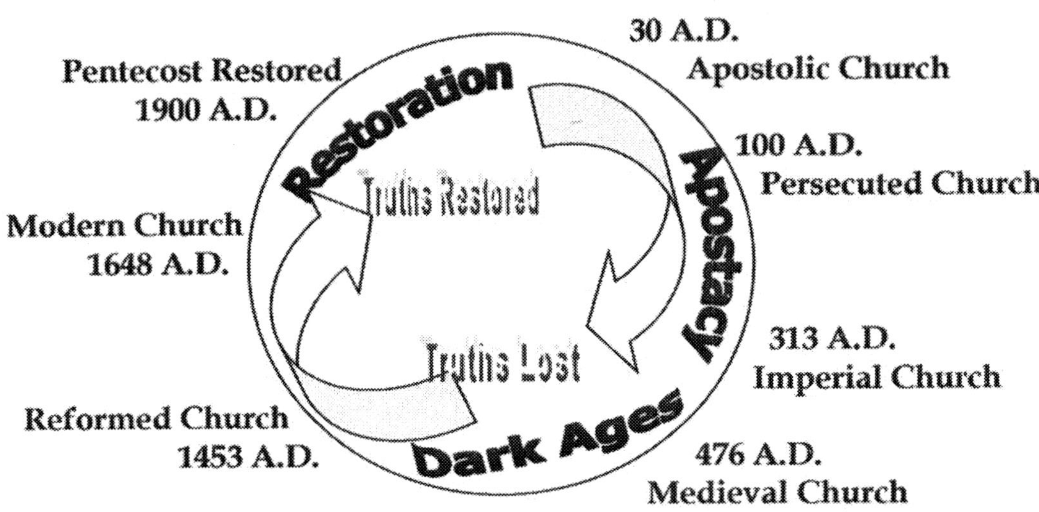

(Reference A.D. Dates from "Present Day Truths" by Dick Iverson with Bill Sheidler)

Restoration, Greek *apokathestemi*, means to restore; literally, it means to set something back again into its original order. Other connotations are: to be completed, to finish, to make prosperous, to recompense, to rescue, to refresh, to set again, to retrieve, to cause to return or to renew. *Restoration refers to the putting back into existence or to use that which has been lost, misplaced, or stolen*, such as principles and truths that were known, believed, taught, and experienced by the early church, rebuilding the foundation of the early apostles and prophets.

> And are built upon the foundation of the apostles and prophets, Jesus Christ himself being the chief corner stone.
>
> —Ephesians 2:20

> According to the grace of God which is given unto me, as a wise masterbuilder, I have laid the foundation, and another buildeth thereon. But let every man take heed how he buildeth thereupon.
>
> —1 Corinthians 3:10

Restoration involves a completion of God's plan of the ages. It involves bringing into existence of those things foretold by the prophets. All that God has said, He will do. This involves a restoration that ends up at the tree of life.

> Repent ye therefore, and be converted, that your sins may be blotted out, when *the times of refreshing* shall come from the presence of the Lord; And he shall send Jesus Christ, which before was preached unto you: Whom heaven must receive until *the times of restitution of all things, which God hath spoken by the mouth of all his holy prophets since the world began.* For Moses truly said unto the fathers, A prophet shall the Lord your God raise up unto you of your brethren like unto me; him shall ye hear in all things whatsoever he shall say unto you. And it shall come to pass, that every soul, which will not hear that prophet shall be destroyed from among the people. Yea, and *all the prophets from Samuel and those that follow after, as many as have spoken, have likewise foretold of these days.*
>
> —Acts 3:19–24, emphasis added

> But now is made manifest, and *by the scriptures of the prophets,* according to the commandment of the everlasting God, made known to all nations for the obedience of faith.
>
> —Romans 16:26, emphasis added

Restitution, Greek *apokatastasis,* is from *apo,* back or again, and *kathistemi,* to set in order, restoration.

> Repent ye therefore, and be converted, that your sins may be blotted out, when *the times of refreshing* shall come from the presence of the Lord; And he shall send Jesus Christ, which before was preached unto you: Whom the heaven must receive *until the times of restitution of all things, which God hath spoken by the mouth of all his holy prophets since the world began.*
>
> —Acts 3:19–21, emphasis added

The following list records the various church ages and acknowledges individuals who were important during each age.

PERSONAGES DURING THE CHURCH AGE

"Departure from truth leads to a decline in power, glory and influence. Carnality, compromise, self-will, worldliness, idolatry, immorality and lukewarmness would be contributing factors in the Church's departure from the **faith** and a corruption of the truths entrusted to the Church." Kevin Conner, "**Restoration Theology**" p. 10.

"It is surely a serious thing of accusing God of withdrawing the Gifts of the Holy Spirit when the Church lost them because of their own lukewarmness. . .The gifts have never entirely ceased. Irenaeus, Tertullian, Chrysostum, Augustine, all refer to these gifts as being still existent in their own times." Donald Gee, "**Concerning Spiritual Gifts**," p. 10

Irenaeus, a student of Polycarp, who was a disciple of the apostle John wrote in his book "Against Heresies," Book V, vi: "In like manner do we also hear many brethren in the church who possess prophetic gifts, and who through the Spirit speak all kinds of languages, and bring to light for the general benefit the hidden things of men and declare the mysteries of God, whom also the apostles term 'spiritual.'" Carl Brumback, "**What Meaneth This**," p. 90.

Tertullian, a great African theologian, who has only one definite and positive reference to ***glossolalia***, was a Montanist. In his famous treatise "Against Marcion" he cited the evidences of spiritual gifts as a proof of God's oneness and as a refutation of Marcion's doctrine of two gods—the God of Wrath in the Old Testament and the God of Love revealed in Jesus of Nazareth. He concluded this argument with a challenge: "Let Marcion then exhibit, as gifts of his god, some prophets, such as have not spoken by human sense, but with the Spirit of God, such as have both predicted things to come, and have made manifest the secrets of the heart; let him produce a psalm, a vision, a prayer—only let it be by the Spirit, in an ecstasy, that is in a rapture, whenever an interpretation of tongues has occurred to him." Glenn Hinson, "**Glossolalia**," p. 50.

Origen, considered the greatest Christian scholar of his age, became president of the catechetical school of Alexandria. In his famous apology, he had to reply to the pagan philosopher Celsus' charge, evidently aimed at Montanist seers, that some Christian prophets uttered all sorts of non-sense. They made exaggerated claims about themselves, asserted Celsus saying: "I am God; I am the Son of God; or I am the Divine Spirit; I have come because the world is perishing, and you, O men, are perishing for your iniquities. But I wish to save you, and you shall see me returning again with heavenly power. Blessed is he who does me homage. . ." Celsus continued, they added "strange, fanatical, and quite unintelligible words, of which no rational person have no meaning at all; but they give occasion to every foul or imposter to apply them to suit his own purposes." Glen Hinson, "**Glossolalia**," p. 51.

Augustine said: "We still do what the apostles did when they laid hands on the Samaritans and called down the Holy Spirit on them by the laying on of hands. It is expected that converts should speak with new tongues." Carl Brumbach, "**What Meaneth This**," p. 91.

Persecuted Church	**100**	**313**
Ignatius	30	107
Polycarp	70	156
Justin Martyr	100	160
Irenaeus	125	203
Tertullian	160	220
Origen	183	254
Cyprian	200	260

Novatian	230	265
Eusebius	263	339
Anathasius	296	373
Imperial Church	**313**	**476**
Basil of Caesarea	320	379
Gregory of Nazianzen	330	389
Gregory of Nyssa	330	395
Ambrose	339	397
Jerome	345	420
Augustine	354	430
John Chrysostom	374	407
Cyril of Alexandria	380	440
The Medieval Church	**476**	**1453**
Gregory the Great	540	604
John of Damascus	675	749
Anselm	1033	1109
Bernard of Clairvaux	1091	1153
Peter Lombard	1095	1159
Peter Waldo	d. ca.	1217
Francis of Assisi	1181	1226
Thomas Aquinas	1225	1274
Meister Eckhart	1260	1327
Johann Tanler	1290	1361
William of Occam	1300	1349
John Wycliffe	1328	1384
John Huss	1369	1415
Thomas A. Kempis	1380	1471
Reformed Church	**1453**	**1648**
Girolamo Savonarola	1452	1498
Desiderius Erasmus	1466	1536
William Tyndale	1494	1536
Martin Luther	1483	1546
Philip Malanchthon	1497	1560
John Calvin	1509	1564
Ulrich Zwingli	1484	1531
John Knox	1513	1572
Conrad Grebel	1498	1526
Francis Xavier	1506	1552

Menno Simons	1496	1561
Thomas Cranmer	1489	1556
Ignatius Loyola	1491	1556
Hugh Latimer	1485	1555
Miles Coverdale	1488	1568
Jacobus Arminius	1560	1609
Thomas Cartwright	1535	1603
Johann Arndt	1555	1621
Robert Browne	1550	1633
Oliver Cromwell	1599	1658
Jon Amos Comenius	1592	1670
Jean Daille	1594	1670
Roger Williams	1603	1683
John Owen	1616	1683
John Bunyan	1628	1688
George Fox	1642	1691
Modern Church	**1648**	**1900**
Madam Guyon	1648	1717
Philip Jacob Spener	1635	1703
August Hermann Francke	1663	1727
David Brainerd	1718	1747
Johanes Albrecht Bengel	1687	1752
Jonathan Edwards	1703	1758
Count von Zinendorf	1700	1760
William Law	1686	1761
John Wesley	1702	1791
George Whitefield	1714	1770
Francis Asbury	1745	1816
William Carey	1761	1834
David Livingstone	1813	1873
Charles Finney	1792	1875
John Nelson Darby	1800	1882
John Henry Newman	1801	1890
Charles Spurgeon	1834	1892
George Muller	1805	1898
Dwight L. Moody	1837	1899
Hudson Taylor	1832	1905
Andrew Murray	1828	1917

Pentecost Restored	**1900**	**Present**
Watchman Nee	1903	1972
Evan Roberts	1878	1951
(1904-1905 Welch Revival)		
William Seymour	1870	1922
(1906-1909 Azusa St. Revival)		
Korean Revival (1907-1910)	1907	1910
Rees Howells	1915	1920
(Southern Africa)		
C. T. Studd	1860	1931
(Belgian Congo)	1913	1931
Billy Graham	1918	2010
(Crusades and Association)	**1947**	**Present**
East African Revival	1920s	1930s
Duncan Campbell	1898	1972
(Hebrides Islands, Scotland)	1949	
Edward Miller	1949	1951
(Argentina Revival, City Bell)		
Reinhard Bonnke (Evangelist: Africa)	**1967**	**Present**
(Founder: Christ for All Nations)		
Revival of Asbury College	1970s	1980s
(Wilmore, Kentucky)		
Muri Thompson	1970	
(Solomon Islands)		
Todd Burke	1973	
(Phnom Penh, Cambodia)		
Papua New Guinea	1973	
(Enga District)		
(Min District)	1977	
John Wimber	1977	
(Vineyard Christian Fellowships)		
Aborigines Revival	1979	
(Elcho Island, Australia)		
Rodney Howard-Browne	1979	
(Evangelistic Ministry)		
Ray Overend	1984	
(Brugam, Papua New Guinea)		
Carlos Annacondia	1985	
(Argentina Revival)		
Claudio Freidzon	1985	
(Argentina Revival)		

Jobson Misang	1988
(North Solomon Islands)	
Johan van Bruggen	1988
(Kambaidam, Papua New Guinea)	
Revival in Madruga, Cuba	1988
Revival in Henan and Anhul, China	1989
Neil Miers, Brisbane, Australia	1993
John Arnot/Randy Clark	1994
(Melbourne, Florida)	
(Eleanor Mumford, Brompton, London) 1994	1994
Ken Gott, Sunderland, England	1994
Randy Clark, Melbourne, Florida	1995
Glenn Berteau, Modesto, California	1995
Brownwood Texas College	1995
Steve Hill, Pensacola, Florida	1995

Since 1995 literally hundreds of local churches in various dimensions all over the world have been experiencing revival of God's glory and power. Awakenings or revivals involve the restoration of truths that have been lost or truths that God wants to make known and strengthen the church by experience.

> O LORD, I have heard thy speech, and was afraid: O LORD, *revive thy work in the midst of the years*, in the midst of the years make known; in wrath remember mercy.
>
> —HABAKKUK 3:2, EMPHASIS ADDED

SIGNIFICANT REVIVALS SINCE AD 1500

Last truth lost *becomes* first truth restored.

						Spontaneous Outpouring of the	New Truths restored: *Laying on of Hands*	
Faith 1517 Reformation	**Water Baptism** 1531 Anabaptists		**Holiness** 1738	**Healing** A. B. Simpson 1840		**Holy Spirit** *begins Topeka, Kansas Bethel Home* Jan. 1, 1901	**Praise & Worship** *Fivefold Ministries End-Time Purposes* 1948	
Luther	Calvin	Arminius	Wesley	Whitefield	Finney	Moody	Sunday	Graham
1483-1546	1509-1564	1560-1609	1703-1791 John 1707-1788 Charles	1714-1770	1792-1875	1837-1899	1862-1925	1918-Present

The Great Welch Revival
Evan Roberts
1904-1905

Azusa Street Revival
William Seymour
April 16, 1906

Martin Luther, Apostle of Faith
The Word of God "The Just shall live by Faith"
The Priesthood of Believers
The Centrality of Preaching
Evangelism

John Calvin, Apostle of Grace
Sovereignty of God
Hopelessness of Man
Adequacy of Christ
Grace Bestowed by Divine Election

James Arminius, Apostle of Grace and Faith
Freedom of the Will
Necessity of Faith for Salvation
The Interlocking of Faith and Grace
Faith and Grace produces Sanctification
Work of the Holy Spirit to Maintain Spiritual Life

John and Charles Wesley, Apostles of Holiness
Freewill and Free Grace
Experiential Conversion
Priesthood of All Believers
Moral Perfection

George Whitefield, Apostle of Humility
Calvinist Who Preached Like an Arminian
Sermons to the Common Man
Powers of Oratory - Voice Lovely and Lively
Fed Hundreds of Hungry People Daily
Great Concern and Care for Orphans

Charles Grandison Finney, Apostle of Sanctification
Separation from Worldliness
Radical Change in Heart
Sanctification by Faith
Necessity of the Power of the Holy Spirit
Union of Man's Will and God's Grace toward Consecration

Dwight L. Moody, Apostle of Cooperative Evangelism
Team Evangelism - Linked Preaching and Music
Man of one Book, the Bible His Sole Authority

Billy Sunday, Apostle of the Sawdust Trail
Backbone of Success: Great Organization
Acrobatic Evangelism: Skipped, Ran, Walked, Bounced, Slid, Gyrated on the Platform.
Preaching: Biting, Blistering, Condemnation of Sin

Billy Graham, Apostle of Team Evangelism
Confidence in Absolute Authority of the Bible
The Weapon: The Sword of the Spirit
The Handle: "The Bible Says"
Train Workers in Personal Evangelism
Adapt to Trends of the Times
Relevant To Complex Problems of Today

Signs of the Second Coming of the Lord Jesus Christ

That we are living in the last of the last days is readily apparent from the signs of the times that are brought to our attention every day by the news media.

> The Pharisees also with the Sadducees came, and tempting desired him that he would shew them a sign from heaven. He answered and said unto them, When it is evening, ye say, It will be fair weather: for the sky is red. And in the morning, It will be foul weather to day: for the sky is red and lowering. O ye hypocrites, ye can discern the face of the sky; but can ye not discern the signs of the times?
>
> —Matthew 16:1–3

Today we have a common saying: Red skies at night, sailor's delight. Red skies in the morning, sailor's warning. Signs of fair weather or inclement weather are made known to the children of men.

> Howbeit that was not first which is spiritual, but that which is natural; and afterward that which is spiritual.
>
> —1 Corinthians 15:46

From Scripture we understand the principle: *first the natural, then the spiritual.* Just as there are natural signs that should motivate us, the Bible gives us spiritual signs to motivate us to follow the guidance of Scripture.

> This know also, that *in the last days perilous times shall come.* For men shall be lovers of their own selves, covetous, boasters, proud, blasphemers, disobedient to parents, unthankful, unholy, Without natural affection, trucebreakers, false accusers, incontinent, fierce, despisers of those that are good, Traitors, heady, highminded, lovers of pleasures more than lovers of God; Having a form of godliness, but denying the power thereof: *from such turn away* [Gr. *apotrepo*, to shun or avoid].
>
> —2 Timothy 3:1–5, emphasis added

The admonition is to shun or avoid such people. In other words, don't chum around or befriend those who live ungodly lives.

> Be ye not unequally yoked together with unbelievers: for what fellowship hath righteousness with unrighteousness? and what communion hath light with darkness? And what concord hath Christ with Belial? or what part hath he that believeth with an infidel? And what agreement hath the temple of God with idols? for *ye are the temple of the living God*; as God hath said, I will dwell in them, and walk in them; and I will be their God, and they shall be my people. Wherefore come out from among them, and be ye separate, saith the Lord, and touch not the unclean thing; and I will receive you, And will be a Father unto you, and ye shall be my sons and daughters, saith the Lord Almighty.
>
> —2 Corinthians 6:14–18, emphasis added

Yet today *all creation* is also urging a transition to the last day:

> For the earnest expectation of the *creature* [Gr. *ktisis*, creation or things created] waiteth for the manifestation of the sons of God. For the creature was made subject to vanity, not willingly, but by reason of him who hath subjected the same in hope, Because the creature itself also shall be delivered

> from the bondage of corruption into the glorious liberty of the children of God. *For we know that the whole creation groaneth and travaileth in pain together until now.* And not only they, but ourselves also, which have the firstfruits of the Spirit, *even we ourselves groan within ourselves, waiting for the adoption, to wit, the redemption of our body.*
>
> —ROMANS 8:19–23, EMPHASIS ADDED

Just read and heed the following warnings by Jesus to His disciples:

> And Jesus answered and said unto them, Take heed that no man deceive you. For many shall come in my name, saying, I am Christ; and shall deceive many. And ye shall hear of wars and rumours of wars: see that ye be not troubled: for all these things must come to pass, but the end is not yet. For nation shall rise against nation, and kingdom against kingdom: and there shall be famines, and pestilences, and earthquakes, in divers (various) places. All these are the beginning of sorrows. Then shall they deliver you up to be afflicted, and shall kill you: and ye shall be hated of all nations for my name's sake. And then shall many be offended, and shall betray one another, and shall hate one another. And many false prophets shall rise, and shall deceive many. And because iniquity shall abound, the love of many shall wax cold. But he that shall endure unto the end, the same shall be saved. And this gospel of the kingdom shall be preached in all the world for a witness unto all nations; and then shall the end come.
>
> —MATTHEW 24:4–14, EMPHASIS ADDED

> And *great earthquakes* shall be in divers [various] places, and famines, and pestilences; and fearful sights and *great signs shall there be from heaven.*
>
> —LUKE 21:11, EMPHASIS ADDED

> And there shall be *signs in the sun, and in the moon, and in the stars; and upon the earth distress of nations, with perplexity* [Gr. from *aporeo*, not to know which way to turn]; *the sea and the waves roaring; Men's hearts failing them for fear,* and for looking after those things which are coming on the earth: for the powers of *heaven shall be shaken.* And *then shall they see the Son of man coming in a cloud with power and great glory.* And when these things begin to come to pass, then look up, and lift up your heads; for *your redemption draweth nigh.*
>
> —LUKE 21:25–28, EMPHASIS ADDED

The prophet Daniel said: "*How great are his signs*! And *how mighty are his wonders*! His kingdom is an everlasting kingdom, and his dominion is from generation to generation" (Dan. 4:3, emphasis added).

The Last One-Half Week of Daniel's Seventy Weeks Prophecy

The coming of the Lord will take place at the end of Daniel's seventy weeks prophecy. As was mentioned previously, Daniel had been instructed to "*shut up the words, and seal the book, even to the time of the end*: many shall run to and fro, and knowledge shall be increased" (Dan. 12:4). And in the same message he instructed, "Go thy way, Daniel: *for the words are closed up and sealed till the time of the end.*" (v. 9, emphasis added).

The vision of the last half week (three and one-half years) of Daniel's seventy weeks prophecy would not occur until the words of the book were opened.

> But thou, O Daniel, shut up the words, and seal the book, *even to the time of the end*: many shall run to and fro, and knowledge shall be increased.
>
> —Daniel 12:4, emphasis added

> And I saw another mighty angel come down from heaven, clothed with a cloud: and a rainbow was upon his head, and his face was as it were the sun, and his feet as pillars of fire: And *he had in his hand a little book open*: and he set his right foot upon the sea, and his left foot on the earth, And cried with a loud voice, as when a lion roareth: and when he had cried, seven thunders uttered their voices. And when the seven thunders had uttered their voices, I was about to write: and I heard a voice from heaven saying unto me, Seal up those things which the seven thunders uttered, and write them not. And the angel which I saw stand upon the sea and upon the earth lifted up his hand to heaven, And sware by him that liveth for ever and ever, who created heaven, and the things that therein are, and the earth, and the things that therein are, and the sea, and the things which are therein, that there should be time no longer [no longer delay]: But in the days of the voice of the seventh angel, when he shall begin to sound, the mystery of God should be finished, as he hath declared to his servants the prophets. And the voice which I heard from heaven spake unto me again, and said, Go and take *the little book which is open* in the hand of the angel which standeth upon the sea and upon the earth. And I went unto the angel, and said unto him, Give me the little book. And he said unto me, Take it, and eat it up; and it shall make thy belly bitter, but it shall be in thy mouth sweet as honey. And I took the little book out of the angel's hand, and ate it up; and it was in my mouth sweet as honey: and as soon as I had eaten it, my belly was bitter. And he said unto me, *Thou must prophesy again before many peoples, and nations, and tongues, and kings.*
>
> —Revelation 10:1–11, emphasis added

Kevin Conner, in his book *The Book of Daniel: An Exposition*, states:

> A contrast and comparison between Daniel and Revelation will unmistakably and wonderfully confirm that "the little OPEN book" that John was told to eat is none other than "the book of Daniel," or more especially that which was sealed to Daniel. The little book open that John eats is the "little book" closed of Daniel.[4]

The mighty angel that had the *little book open* directs John to eat it up for the time had come for John to prophesy the contents of Daniel's shut up and sealed book.

> And he swore by him who lives for ever and ever, who created the heavens and all that is in them, the earth and all that is in it, and the sea and all that is in it, that there would be no more delay.
>
> —Revelation 10:6, esv, emphasis added

After John had eaten the *little open book*, the angel tells John: "Thou must prophesy again before many peoples, and nations, and tongues, and kings" (Rev. 10:11).

It is at this time, after eating the opened little book, which Daniel was told to shut up the words and seal the book, that John sees clearly to prophesy events that will occur in the next three and one-half years (*the period of the great tribulation*). John begins to prophecy the last half of Daniel's seventieth week in *Revelation 11* (*42 months* in verse 1 and *1260 days* in verse 3), *Revelation 12* (*1260 days* in verse 6 and *time, times, and half a time* in verse 14), and *Revelation 13* (*forty-two months* in verse 5)—all of which equal *three and one-half years* (the last one-half week) *concluding the seventy weeks prophecy in Daniel 9.* John then continues the prophetic events of Daniel's last one-half week from Revelation 11 up to and including the Second Coming of Jesus in Revelation 19.

The Great Tribulation

There are waves of tribulation going on immediately prior to the "Great Tribulation," which includes the *seven seal judgments* and the *first six trumpet judgments.*

The Great Tribulation occurs before the Second Coming of the Lord Jesus Christ. Nothing compares to this dark hour of world history during the reign of the Antichrist. It is the period of time during the blowing of the seventh trumpet when the seven vials (bowls) of God's wrath are being poured out upon the earth.

> And I heard a great voice out of the temple saying to the seven angels, Go your ways, and pour out the vials of the wrath of God upon the earth. And the first went, and poured out his vial upon the earth; and there fell a noisome and grievous sore upon the men which had the mark of the beast, and upon them which worshipped his image. And the second angel poured out his vial upon the sea; and it became as the blood of a dead man: and every living soul died in the sea. And the third angel poured out his vial upon the rivers and fountains of waters; and they became blood. And I heard the angel of the waters say, Thou art righteous, O Lord, which art, and wast, and shalt be, because thou hast judged thus. For they have shed the blood of saints and prophets, and thou hast given them blood to drink; for they are worthy. And I heard another out of the altar say, Even so, Lord God Almighty, true and righteous are thy judgments. And the fourth angel poured out his vial upon the sun; and power was given unto him to scorch men with fire. And men were scorched with great heat, and blasphemed the name of God, which hath power over these plagues: and they repented not to give him glory. And the fifth angel poured out his vial upon the seat of the beast; and his kingdom was full of darkness; and they gnawed their tongues for pain, And blasphemed the God of heaven because of their pains and their sores, and repented not of their deeds. And the sixth angel poured out his vial upon the great river Euphrates; and the water thereof was dried up, that the way of the kings of the east might be prepared. And I saw three unclean spirits like frogs come out of the mouth of the dragon, and out of the mouth of the beast, and out of the mouth of the false prophet. For they are the spirits of devils, working miracles, which go forth unto the kings of the earth and of the whole world, to gather them to the battle of that great day of God Almighty. Behold, I come as a thief. Blessed is he that watcheth, and keepeth his garments, lest he walk naked, and they see his shame. And he gathered them together into a place called in the Hebrew tongue Armageddon. And the seventh angel poured out his vial into the air; and there came a great voice out of the temple of heaven, from the throne, saying, It is done.
>
> —Revelation 16:1–17

Daniel declares that nothing compares to this time of trouble since there was a nation, but that during that time "*thy people shall be delivered*" (everyone found written in the book).

> And at that time shall Michael stand up, the great prince which standeth for the children of thy people: and there shall be a time of trouble, such as never was since there was a nation [even] to that same time: *and at that time thy people shall be delivered, every one that shall be found written in the book.*
>
> —Daniel 12:1, emphasis added

"But *ye, brethren, are not in darkness, that that day should overtake you as a thief.* Ye are all the children of light, and the children of the day: we are not of the night, nor of darkness. Therefore let us not sleep, as do others; but let us watch and be sober. For they that sleep sleep in the night; and they that be drunken are drunken in the night. But let us, who are of the day, be sober, putting on the breastplate of faith and love; and for an helmet, the hope of salvation. *For God hath not appointed us to wrath, but to obtain salvation by our Lord Jesus Christ,* Who died for us, that, whether we wake or sleep, we should live together with him. Wherefore comfort yourselves together, and edify one another, even as also ye do.

—1 Thessalonians 5:4–11, emphasis added

The Antichrist

Although there are many antichrists in the world (those against Christ) and there is a "spirit of antichrist" (1 John 4:3), there is also *a future individual* who is called *the Antichrist.* Today, the spirit of antichrist works in the unbelieving world and also within those who are apostates from Christianity—those who have "fallen away" from the faith.

Let no man deceive you by any means: for that day shall not come, except there come a falling away first, and that man of sin be revealed, the son of perdition.

—2 Thessalonians 2:3

And he shall speak great words against the most High, and shall wear out the saints of the most High, and think to change times and laws: and they shall be given into his hand until a time and times and the dividing of time.

—Daniel 7:25

And there was given unto him a mouth speaking great things and blasphemies; and power was given unto him to continue forty and two months. And he opened his mouth in blasphemy against God, to blaspheme his name, and his tabernacle, and them that dwell in heaven. And it was given unto him to make war with the saints, and to overcome them: and power was given him over all kindreds, and tongues, and nations.

—Revelation 13:5–7

And the holy city shall they tread under foot forty and two months.

Revelation 11:2d

Resurrection and Rapture

The expression, "the church," isn't mentioned in Revelation from Revelation 4:1 to Revelation 19. However, believers *are* mentioned throughout Revelation, as it is said, "Consistency thou art a jewel!" In the New Testament the mere mention of "the saints" is to mention the church of the Lord Jesus. *Saints* refers to *all believers.* The word *church* is also not mentioned in the following books of the New Testament: 2 Peter, 1 John, 2 John, and Jude. But will one argue those books are not directed to the church? There is but *one body* of believers:

To the church of God which is at Corinth, *to* those who have been sanctified in Christ Jesus, *saints by calling* [holy ones] with *all* who *in every place call on the name of our Lord Jesus Christ*, their Lord and ours.

—1 Corinthians 1:2, NAS, emphasis added

There is one body, and one Spirit, even as ye are called in one hope of your calling; One Lord, one faith, one baptism, One God and Father of all, who is above all, and through all, and in you all.

—Ephesians 4:4–5

Paul, an apostle of Christ Jesus by the will of God, To the *saints* who are at Ephesus *and who are faithful in Christ Jesus.*

—Ephesians 1:1, emphasis added

And when he had opened the fifth seal, I saw under the altar *the souls of them that were slain for the word of God*, and *for the testimony which they held*: And they cried with a loud voice, saying, How long, O Lord, holy and true, dost thou not judge and avenge our blood on them that dwell on the earth? *And white robes were given unto every one of them*; and it was said unto them, that they should rest yet for a little season, until their fellowservants also and their brethren, that should be killed as they were, should be fulfilled.

—Revelation 6:9–11, emphasis added

And one of the elders answered, saying unto me, *What are these which are arrayed in white robes? and whence came they? And I said unto him, Sir, thou knowest. And he said to me, These are they which came out of great tribulation, and have washed their robes, and made them white in the blood of the Lamb.* Therefore are they before the throne of God, and serve him day and night in his temple: and he that sitteth on the throne shall dwell among them. They shall hunger no more, neither thirst any more; neither shall the sun light on them, nor any heat. For the Lamb which is in the midst of the throne shall feed them, and shall lead them unto living fountains of waters: and God shall wipe away all tears from their eyes.

—Revelation 7:13–17, emphasis added

And the dragon was wroth with the woman, and went to make war with the remnant of her seed, which keep the commandments of God, and *have the testimony of Jesus Christ.*

—Revelation 12:17, emphasis added

And it was given unto him **to** *make war with the saints*, and to overcome them: and power was given him over all kindreds, and tongues, and nations. And all that dwell upon the earth shall worship him, whose names are not written in the book of life of the Lamb slain from the foundation of the world. If any man have an ear, let him hear. He that leadeth into captivity shall go into captivity: he that killeth with the sword must be killed with the sword. Here is *the patience and the faith of the saints.*

—Revelation 13:7–10, emphasis added

Here is the *patience of the saints: here are they that keep the commandments of God, and the faith of Jesus.* And I heard a voice from heaven saying unto me, Write, *Blessed are the dead which die in the Lord from henceforth*: Yea, saith the Spirit, that they may rest from their labours; and their works do follow them.

—Revelation 14:12–13, emphasis added

> And I heard another voice from heaven, saying, *Come out of her, my people*, that ye be not partakers of her sins, and that ye receive not of her plagues.
>
> —REVELATION 18:4, EMPHASIS ADDED

> Unto him be glory *in the church* by Christ Jesus *throughout all ages, world without end*. Amen.
>
> EPHESIANS 3:21, EMPHASIS ADDED

Under the New Testament economy, to believe in and obey the Lord Jesus Christ is to be part of His body, the church.

The *first resurrection* and the *rapture of the church* are one and the same event.

> Jesus said unto her, *I am the resurrection, and the life*: he that believeth in me, though he were dead, yet shall he live: And whosoever liveth and believeth in me shall never die. Believest thou this?
>
> —JOHN 11:25–26, EMPHASIS ADDED

> And I saw thrones, and they sat upon them, and judgment was given unto them: and I saw the souls of them that were beheaded for the witness of Jesus, and for the word of God, and which had not worshipped the beast, neither his image, neither had received his mark upon their foreheads, or in their hands; and *they lived and reigned with Christ a thousand years*. But the rest of the dead lived not again until the thousand years were finished. *This is the first resurrection*. Blessed and holy is he that hath part in *the first resurrection*: on such the second death hath no power, but *they shall be priests of God and of Christ, and shall reign with him a thousand years*.
>
> —REVELATION 20:4–6, EMPHASIS ADDED

> Now this I say, brethren, that *flesh and blood cannot inherit the kingdom of God*; neither doth corruption inherit incorruption. Behold, I shew you a mystery; We shall not all sleep, but *we shall all be changed, In a moment, in the twinkling of an eye, at the last trump*: for the trumpet shall sound, and the dead shall be raised incorruptible, and we shall be changed. *For this corruptible must put on incorruption, and this mortal must put on immortality*. So when this corruptible shall have put on incorruption, and this mortal shall have put on immortality, then shall be brought to pass the saying that is written, Death is swallowed up in victory.
>
> —1 CORINTHIANS 15:50–54, EMPHASIS ADDED

> And the *seventh angel sounded* [the last trump]; and *there were great voices in heaven*, saying, *The kingdoms of this world are become the kingdoms of our Lord, and of his Christ; and he shall reign for ever and ever*.
>
> —REVELATION 11:15, EMPHASIS ADDED

> But I would not have you to be ignorant, brethren, concerning them which are asleep, that ye sorrow not, even as others which have no hope. For if we believe that Jesus died and rose again, even so them also which sleep in Jesus will God bring with him. For this we say unto you by the word of the Lord, that we which are alive and remain unto the coming of the Lord shall not prevent them which are asleep. *For the Lord himself shall descend from heaven with a shout, with the voice of the archangel, and with the trump of God: and the dead in Christ shall rise first: Then we which are alive and remain shall be caught up together with them in the clouds, to meet the Lord in the air: and so shall we ever be with the Lord*. Wherefore comfort one another with these words.
>
> —1 THESSALONIANS 4:13–18, EMPHASIS ADDED

The following is a numbered sequence of events.

1. The Lord descends from heaven
2. With a shout (Gr. *keleuma*, command or an order given) and with *the voice* (Gr. *phone*, sound or tone) (i.e. sound of uttered words) of the archangel
3. With the trump (or trumpet) of God
4. Resurrection of all the dead in Christ (from Adam to the last saint that died)
5. Every living believer will be changed (change from one thing to another, transformed)
6. A snatching away of all believers who have been resurrected or changed
7. Caught up together with them in the clouds to meet the Lord in the air
8. Every believing saint shall be with the Lord forever

If there was to be a "secret rapture" at the beginning of a seven year great tribulation, then *what about the saints who die within the seven year tribulation period*? It would require another coming of the Lord (another resurrection, another rapture). *How many Second Comings are there to be? Concerning those events the Bible is silent.*

> And as it is appointed unto men once to die, but after this the judgment: So Christ was *once offered to bear the sins of many*; and unto them that look for him shall *he appear the second time without sin unto salvation.*
>
> —HEBREWS 9:27–28, EMPHASIS ADDED

Jesus Christ was *once* offered to bear the sins of many; likewise, unto them that look for him shall He appear *the second time* without sin unto salvation. Therefore, there is but *one second coming.* There will not be two second comings, two first resurrections, or two raptures! Some teach, contrary and erroneously to the Word of God, of a series of progressive raptures and resurrections over a period of seven years tribulation. There is *but one documented first resurrection* (rapture of believers) according to the Bible. Conner explains it thus:

> The resurrection of the dead and the rapture of the living both take place at the actual Second Coming of Christ. The coming of the Lord "for" His saints (the Rapture) and "with" His saints (the Revelation) take place at one and the same period of time.[5]

> And to you who are troubled rest with us, when the Lord Jesus shall be revealed from heaven with his mighty angels, In flaming fire taking vengeance on them that know not God, and that obey not the gospel of our Lord Jesus Christ: Who shall be punished with everlasting destruction from the presence of the Lord, and from the glory of his power; When he shall come to be glorified in his saints, and to be admired in all them that believe (because our testimony among you was believed) *in that day.*
>
> —2 THESSALONIANS 1:7–10, EMPHASIS ADDED

Do you gather from the above scripture that "in that day" that Jesus comes to be glorified in His saints (to be admired in all them that believe) He will also come "in flaming fire taking vengeance on them that know not God, and obey not the gospel of our Lord Jesus Christ" and "who shall be punished with everlasting destruction from the presence of the Lord, and from the glory of his power"? These are *two events in one day.*

> And I saw heaven opened, and behold a white horse; and he that sat upon him was called Faithful and True, and in righteousness he doth judge and make war. His eyes were as a flame of fire, and on his head were many crowns; and he had a name written, that no man knew, but he himself. And he was clothed with a vesture dipped in blood: and his name is called The word of God. And the armies which were in heaven followed him upon white horses, clothed in fine linen, white and clean. And out of his mouth goeth a sharp sword, that with it he should smite the nations: and he shall rule them with a rod of iron: and he treadeth the winepress of the fierceness and wrath of Almighty God. And he hath on his vesture and on his thigh a name written, King Of Kings, And Lord Of Lords. And I saw an angel standing in the sun; and he cried with a loud voice, saying to all the fowls that fly in the midst of heaven, Come and gather yourselves together unto the supper of the great God; That ye may eat the flesh of kings, and the flesh of captains, and the flesh of mighty men, and the flesh of horses, and of them that sit on them, and the flesh of all men, both free and bond, both small and great. And I saw the beast, and the kings of the earth, and their armies, gathered together to make war against him that sat on the horse, and against his army. And the beast was taken, and with him the false prophet that wrought miracles before him, with which he deceived them that had received the mark of the beast, and them that worshipped his image. These both were cast alive into a lake of fire burning with brimstone. And the remnant were slain with the sword of him that sat upon the horse, which sword proceeded out of his mouth: and all the fowls were filled with their flesh.
>
> —Revelation 19:11–21

1. No Secret Rapture

   "Behold, he cometh with clouds; and *every eye shall see him*, and they also which pierced him: and all kindreds of the earth shall wail because of him. Even so, Amen" (Rev. 1:7, emphasis added).

2. Only One Second Coming

   "So Christ was once offered to bear the sins of many; and unto them that look for him shall he appear *the second time* without sin unto salvation" (Heb. 9:28, emphasis added).

3. Christians Suffering under the Wrath of God?

   "For *God hath not appointed us to wrath*, but to obtain salvation by our Lord Jesus Christ" (1 Thess. 5:9, emphasis added).

4. Escape or Persecution during Tribulation?

   "And I saw thrones, and they sat upon them, and judgment was given unto them: and I saw *the souls of them that were beheaded for the witness of Jesus*, and for the word of God, and which had not worshipped the beast, neither his image, neither had

> received his mark upon their foreheads, or in their hands; *and they lived and reigned with Christ a thousand years*" (Rev. 20:4, emphasis added).

The Second Coming of Jesus (Rapture and revelation) occurs just prior to the Millennial Age at which time Satan will be bound in the bottomless pit for one thousand years.

> And not only the creation, but we ourselves, who have the firstfruits of the Spirit, groan inwardly as we wait eagerly for adoption as sons, the redemption of our bodies.
>
> —Romans 8:23, esv

> I tell you this, brothers: flesh and blood cannot inherit the kingdom of God, nor does the perishable inherit the imperishable. Behold! I tell you a mystery. We shall not all sleep, but we shall all be changed, in a moment, in the twinkling of an eye, at the last trumpet. For the trumpet will sound, and the dead will be raised imperishable, and we shall be changed. For this perishable body must put on the imperishable, and this mortal body must put on immortality.
>
> —1 Corinthians 15:50–53, esv

> But we do not want you to be uninformed, brothers, about those who are asleep, that you may not grieve as others do who have no hope. For since we believe that Jesus died and rose again, even so, through Jesus, God will bring with him those who have fallen asleep.[5] For this we declare to you by a word from the Lord, that we who are alive, who are left until the coming of the Lord, will not precede those who have fallen asleep. For the Lord himself will descend from heaven with a cry of command, with the voice of an archangel, and with the sound of the trumpet of God. And the dead in Christ will rise first. Then we who are alive, who are left, will be caught up together with them in the clouds to meet the Lord in the air, and so we will always be with the Lord. Therefore encourage one another with these words.
>
> 1 Thessalonians 4:13–18, esv

Chapter 9
SEEING DAY 7

The Millennium (about 1,000 years)

Blessed and holy is he that hath part in the first resurrection: on such the second death hath no power, but they shall be priests of God and of Christ, and shall reign with him a thousand years.
—Revelation 20:6

The brightest years to come will transform the landscape. The moon will become as bright as the sun in the night skies. Miracle of miracles brought forth by the power of Almighty God, in which the laws of nature will be transformed giving to all the redeemed of past ages a radiance and splendor yet *without* the blistering heat from the sun or hurtful effects from the moon.

That glorious 1,000-year day will be the fulfillment of the Proverb: "But the path of the just is as the shining light, that shineth more and more unto *the perfect day*" (Prov. 4:18, emphasis added).

The Seventh Day (Seventh One Thousand Year Period)

> Moreover, the light of the moon will be like the light of the sun, and the light of the sun will be sevenfold, like the light of seven days [concentrated in one], in the day that the Lord binds up the hurt of His people, and heals their wound [inflicted by Him because of their sins].
>
> —Isaiah 30:26, amp

In the King James Version it reads similarly:

> Moreover the light of the moon shall be as the light of the sun, and the light of the sun shall be sevenfold, *as the light of seven days, in the day that the* Lord [1] bindeth up the breach of his people, and [2] healeth the stroke of their wound.
>
> —Isaiah 30:26, emphasis added

(See Hosea 6:1–4.) Drechsler describes it correctly: "The radiated light, which is sufficient to produce the daylight for a whole week according to the existing order of things, will be concentrated into a single day."[1]

Luther renders it in this way (translated from German) "(as if seven days were enclosed in one another).[2]

Delitzsch and Martin have this comment on the subject:

> This also is not meant figuratively, any more than Paul means is figuratively, when he says, that with the manifestation of the "glory" of the children of God, the "corruption" of universal nature will come to an end. Nevertheless, it is not of the new heaven that the prophet is speaking, but of the

> glorification of nature, which is promised by both the Old Testament prophecy and by that of the New at the closing period of the world's history, and which will be the closing typical self-annunciation of that eternal glory in which everything will be swallowed up.[3]

Notice in the following chart that the overcomer promises in the Book of Revelation are sequential and can be coordinated with the 1,000-year periods throughout God's redemptive week. The *first overcomer promise* begins from Adam to Noah and makes reference to the "*tree of life*."

The second promise from the days of Noah to Abraham making reference to the overcomer *not being hurt of the second death* (*lake of fire*). Contrast this reference with the time of the Flood when all the ungodly perished. Only eight souls were saved during the great deluge.

The *third promise* from the days of Abraham to Samuel reference is made of *the hidden manna and white stone* notable during the days of Moses and the Exodus from Egypt.

The *fourth promise* from the days of Samuel to Christ makes reference to giving the overcomer *power over the nations and the morning star* that speaks of the rulerships of David and Solomon (David established his kingdom to the great river, Euphrates, fulfilling the Abrahamic land promise in Genesis 15.) "I am the root and the offspring of David, and the bright and morning star" (Rev. 22:16). (See also Jeremiah 33:19–21.)

The *fifth promise* begins with Day 5 and due to the sacrificial and vicarious death of Christ, overcomers are *clothed in white raiment* (in other words, declared righteous) and Christ will *confess His name before His Father and the angels.*

The *sixth promise* beginning with Day 6 to Day 7 during which time God is restoring and preparing His bride for his Second Coming. The temple here is the corporate body of Christ. The overcomer is to be *a pillar in the temple and will have written on him a new name.*

The *seventh* promise beginning with Day 7 (the Millennium) at which time overcomers are promised that they will *sit with Him on His throne* (reigning with Him) during the seventh 1,000 years, which will be the Millennium.

The *eighth promise* begins after the creation of the new heaven and new earth and overcomers have a promise to *inherit all things and He will be our God and the overcomer shall be His son.* The number eight is symbolic of new beginnings and here it refers to the overcomer inheriting all things in eternity.

OVERCOMER PROMISES FROM THE BOOK OF REVELATION

DAY 1	DAY 2	DAY 3	DAY 4	DAY 5	DAY 6	DAY 7	ETERNITY
Tree of Life	**Not be hurt of the Second Death**	**Hidden Manna White Stone A New Name**	**Power over the Nations Rule with Rod of Iron Morning Star**	**Clothed with White Raiment Name in Book of Life Confesses Name**	**Pillar in the Temple (Church) Name of the City Name of the Father**	**Throne Kingdom Authority**	**Inherit All Things**
Paradise Lost	The Flood	Moses-White Stone of Betrothal	David/Solomon Authority over Nations	Clothing Adam & Eve Lost	New Jerusalem Bride made herself ready	Dominion Lost/Now Restored	New Heaven and New Earth

1. Revelation 2:7
To him that ***overcometh*** will I give to eat of **the tree of life**, which is in the midst of the paradise of God.

5. Revelation 3:4,5
He that ***overcometh***, the same shall be **clothed in white raiment**; and I will not blot out his name out of the book of life, but I will **confess his name before my** Father, and before his angels.

2. Revelation 2:11
He that ***overcometh*** shall not be hurt of **the second death**.

3. Revelation 2:17
To him that ***overcometh*** will I give to eat of **the hidden manna**, and will give him **a white stone**, and in the stone **a new name written**, which no man knoweth saving he that receiveth it.

6. Revelation 3:12
Him that ***overcometh*** will I make **a pillar in the temple of my God**, and he shall go no more out: and I will **write upon him the name of my God**, and **the name of the city of my God**, which is new Jerusalem. . . And I will write upon him **my new name**.

4. Revelation 2:26-28
And he that ***overcometh***, and keepeth my works unto the end, to him will I give **power over the nations**: And he shall **rule them with a rod of iron**; as the vessels of a potter shall they be broken into shivers: even as I received of my Father. And I will give him **the morning star**.

7. Revelation 3:21
To him that **overcometh** will I grant to sit with me in my throne, even as I also overcame, and am sit down with my Father in his throne.

8. Revelation 21:7
He that ***overcometh*** shall **inherit all things**; and I will be his God, and he shall be my son.

In the following chart we see a breakdown of the light of seven days.

The Light of Seven Days

"The mystery of the seven stars that you saw in my right hand, and of the seven golden lampstands is this: The seven stars are the angels of the seven churches: and the seven lampstands are the seven churches. Revelation 1:20 NIV

"But beloved, be not ignorant of this one thing, that one day is with the Lord as a thousand years, and a thousand years as one day." II Peter 3:8

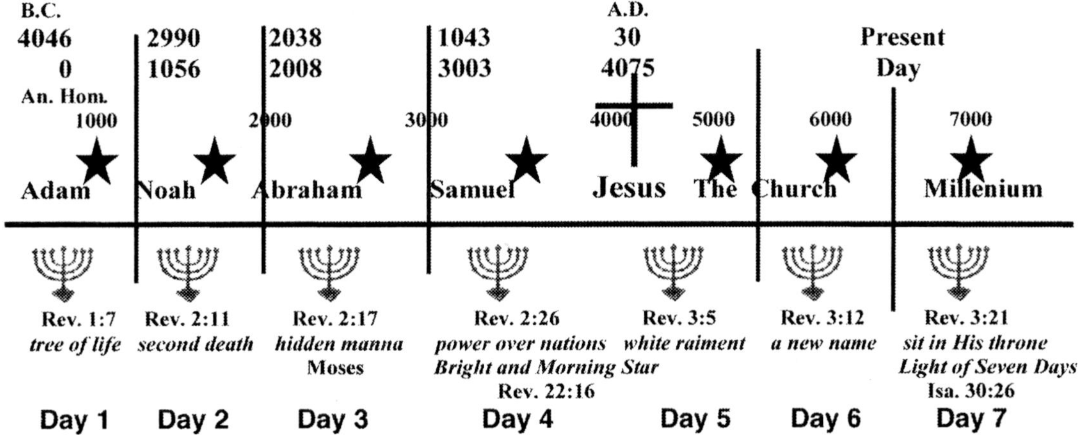

"Moreover the light of the moon shall be as the light of the sun, and the light of the sun shall be sevenfold, as
THE LIGHT OF SEVEN DAYS,
IN THE DAY that the LORD
1. bindeth up the breach of his people, and
2. healeth the stroke of their wound." Isaiah 30:26

"Come, and let us return unto the Lord:
1. for he hath torn, and he will heal us;
2. he hath smitten, and he will bind us up.
After two days will he revive us:
in the third day he will raise us up,
and we shall live in his sight.
Then shall we know if we follow on to know the Lord: his going forth is prepared as the morning; and
he shall come unto us as the rain,
as the latter and former rain unto the earth." Hosea 6:1-3

For a thousand years in thy sight are but as yesterday when it is past, and as a watch in the night. Psalm 90:4

Heaven and earth will be adorned beautifully. It will be the sabbath of the Lord's week of redemption. The light of the seven days of the Lord's week will be concentrated in the seventh day. From the beginning of creation was light, and its close will be light as well. As when the sun today shines at its zenith, it dispels shadows and darkness.

The church is shadowed forth in the Old Testament by that great company which came out of Egypt and made their way into the wilderness, where they were fed and nourished of God for the space of *forty years.*

> This is he, that was in *the church in the wilderness* with the angel which spake to him in the mount Sina, and with our fathers: who received the lively oracles to give unto us:
>
> —Acts 7:38, emphasis added

The tabernacle of witness in the wilderness was also a type of the New Testament church. The cubical measurements of the holy place, 10 X 10 X 20 = 2,000, were significant of the 2,000 years of the church age.

The most holy place, 10 X 10 X 10 = 1,000, foreshadowed the *1,000 years* of the millennial age, in which the tabernacle of God is with men,

> And I heard a great voice out of heaven saying, Behold, *the tabernacle of God is with men*, and he will dwell with them, and they shall be his people, and God himself shall be with them, and be their God.
>
> —Revelation 21:3, emphasis added

Jesus Christ is seen in the midst of His church walking in the midst of His people, clothed in the garments of the Melchizedek priesthood.

> And it is yet far more evident: for that after the similitude of Melchisedec there ariseth another priest, Who is made, not after the law of a carnal commandment, but after the power of an endless life. For he testifieth, Thou art a priest for ever after the order of Melchisedec.
>
> —Hebrews 7:15–17

The six-day period of creation is followed by the seventh day in which God ceases from His work.

> For in six days the Lord made heaven and earth, the sea, and all that in them is, and *rested the seventh day*: wherefore the Lord blessed the sabbath day, and hallowed it.
>
> —Exodus 20:11, emphasis added

God's Lamb was slain from the foundation of the world (Rev. 13:8). He was *not crucified then*, yet He was designated or "kept up" by the Father to be crucified four days or 4,000 years later. Jesus was hidden from man for four days (4,000 years). "No man hath seen God at any time; the only begotten Son, *which is in the bosom of the Father, he hath declared him*" (John 1:18). As Peter says: "But with the precious blood of Christ, as of *a lamb without blemish and without spot*: *Who verily was foreordained before the foundation of the world, but was manifest in these last times for you*" (1 Pet. 1:19–20).

> In the *tenth day of this month they shall take to them every man a lamb*... Your lamb shall be without blemish, a male of the first year: ye shall take it out from the sheep, or from the goats: And ye shall

> *keep it up until the fourteenth day* of the same month: and the whole assembly of the congregation of Israel shall kill it in the evening.
>
> —EXODUS 12:3, 5–6, EMPHASIS ADDED

> When Pilate saw that he could prevail nothing, but that rather a tumult was made, he took water, and washed his hands before the multitude, saying, I am innocent of the blood of this just person: see ye to it. *Then answered all the people, and said, His blood be on us, and on our children.*
>
> —MATTHEW 27:24–25, EMPHASIS ADDED

The seven one thousand years days of the Lord are comprised of *four days*: *day one* (1,000 years) from Adam to Noah, *day two* (1,000 years) from Noah to Abram, *day three*, (1,000 years) from Abram to Samuel, *day four* (1,000 years) from Samuel to Messiah (the Lord Jesus Christ), *days five and six* (2,000 years) of the Church Age, and the last day, *day seven*, the Millennium (1,000 years). [Hosea gives a prophetic glimpse of the church age and the millennial age, "after two days" (2,000 years), and "on the third day" (1,000 years).]

> After two days He will revive us; On the third day He will raise us up, That we may live in His sight.
>
> —HOSEA 6:2, NKJV, EMPHASIS ADDED

After two days of the church age, at the end of which, it seems certain that many in natural Israel shall see the light of the Messiah and be grafted back into the olive tree (Rom. 11:24, 26).

> I say then, Have they stumbled that they should fall? God forbid: but rather through their fall salvation is come unto the Gentiles, for to provoke them to jealousy. Now if the fall of them be the riches of the world, and the diminishing of them the riches of the Gentiles; how much more their fulness?
>
> —ROMANS 11:11–12

The one day of the millennial age (the 1,000 years) is the seventh day of God's redemptive work, the last day, the millennial sabbath of rest, is spoken of in Hebrews 4:9 where the writer says "there remains therefore a rest [Gr. *sabbatismos*, literally "the keeping of a sabbath"] for the people of God" (NKJV).

The believer has already entered and experiences "His rest." However, this *sabbatismos* is *the rest after the six days of God's work of redemption*, where there is no sin, no sickness, no death, and no devil working contrary to believers (the church). And there is also a sabbath rest for creation:

> For the earnest expectation of the *creature* [Gr. *ktisis*, things created] waiteth for the manifestation of the sons of God. For the creature was made subject to vanity, not willingly, but by reason of him who hath subjected the same in hope, *Because the creature itself also shall be delivered from the bondage of corruption into the glorious liberty of the children of God*. For we know that *the whole creation* groaneth and travaileth in pain together until now. And not only they, but ourselves also, which have the firstfruits of the Spirit, even we ourselves groan within ourselves, waiting for the adoption, to wit, the redemption of our body. For we are saved by hope: but hope that is seen is not hope: for what a man seeth, why doth he yet hope for?
>
> —ROMANS 8:19–24, EMPHASIS ADDED

Creation also will be delivered from "the bondage of corruption into the glorious liberty of the children of God" in this brand-new 1,000-year redemption day of rest.

The same day of the Second Coming we see *two things* happening:

> And to you who are troubled rest with us, when the Lord Jesus shall be revealed from heaven with his mighty angels, [1] In flaming fire taking vengeance on them that know not God, and that obey not the gospel of our Lord Jesus Christ: Who shall be punished with everlasting destruction from the presence of the Lord, and from the glory of his power; [2] *When* he shall come to be glorified in his saints, and to be admired in all them that believe (because our testimony among you was believed) *in that day.*
>
> — 2 Thessalonians 1:7–10, emphasis added

> Now this I say, brethren, that flesh and blood cannot inherit the kingdom of God; neither doth corruption inherit incorruption. Behold, I shew you a mystery; We shall not all sleep, but we shall all be changed, In a moment, in the twinkling of an eye, *at the last trump*: for the trumpet shall sound, and the dead shall be raised incorruptible, and we shall be changed. For this corruptible must put on incorruption, and this mortal must put on immortality. So when this corruptible shall have put on incorruption, and this mortal shall have put on immortality, then shall be brought to pass the saying that is written, Death is swallowed up in victory.
>
> —1 Corinthians 15:50–54, emphasis added

This begins the millennial rest day, the seventh day of God's redemptive week. This day is designated as mainly a keeping of sabbath rest.

Various Renderings of Hebrews 4:9

- KJV: "There remaineth therefore a rest to the people of God."
- ESV: "So then, there remains a Sabbath rest for the people of God."
- AMP: "So then, there is still awaiting a full and complete Sabbath-rest reserved for the [true] people of God."
- GW: "Therefore, a time of rest and worship exists for God's people."
- NAS: http://biblehub.com/nasb/hebrews/4.htm "So there remains a Sabbath rest for the people of God."
- EXB: "This shows that the ·rest [Sabbath rest; sharing in the rest God enjoyed after Creation] for God's people ·is still coming [or is still available; remains]."
- Phillips: "There still exists, therefore, a full and complete rest for the people of God."

Strong's Definition of "sabbath rest" in Hebrews 4:9: SC 04520 *sabbatismos*: (1) a keeping Sabbath; (2) the blessed rest from toils and troubles looked for in the age to come by the true worshippers of God and true Christians.[4]

Believers in the seventh 1,000-year millennium will have *glorified bodies and they will reign with Christ*. This time is yet future. From the beginning of time the kingdom (or sphere of God's rule) is *from heaven* extending over angels, humans, and all created things. The kingdom of God is *within* for believers and only comes to one by faith and obedience. Righteousness, peace and joy in the Holy Ghost (Rom. 14:17) is the nature of those who by faith and obedience enter God's kingdom. Natural Israel (and even the disciples) looked for an outward, physical, economic, political, and materialistic kingdom that they believed Christ would set up on this earth. Their spiritual senses were dulled by not understanding. God's rule and reign is from heaven, as always. Matthew 21:43 tells us, "Therefore say I unto you, The kingdom of God shall be taken from you, and *given to a nation bringing forth the fruits thereof*" (emphasis added). Because of unbelief the kingdom of God was taken from natural Israel and given to a holy nation.

> But ye are a chosen generation, a royal priesthood, *an holy nation*, a peculiar people; that ye should shew forth the praises of him who hath called you out of darkness into his marvellous light: *Which in time past were not a people, but are now the people of God: which had not obtained mercy, but now have obtained mercy.*
>
> —1 PETER 2:9–10, EMPHASIS ADDED

This holy nation is comprised of believers, *both Jew and Gentile*. These are those, who with glorified bodies, will enter into the Millennium for 1,000 years to reign with Christ.

> Unto him be glory *in the church* by Christ Jesus throughout all ages [successive generations], *world* [perpetuity of time, eternity] without end [in other words, forever]. Amen.
>
> —EPHESIANS 3:21, EMPHASIS ADDED

The kingdom that Jesus proclaimed was a spiritual kingdom in the hearts of believing men and women, here and now. Believers are governed by the laws of the kingdom, as spoken in the Sermon on the Mount (Matthew 5–7). Jesus said, "Upon this rock I will build my church...and I will give you the *keys of the kingdom*" (Matt. 6:18–19, emphasis added).

> But now in Christ Jesus ye who sometimes were far off are made nigh by the blood of Christ. *For he is our peace, who hath made both one, and hath broken down the middle wall of partition between us*; Having abolished in his flesh the enmity, even the law of commandments contained in ordinances; *for to make in himself of twain one new man*, so making peace; And that he might *reconcile both unto God in one body by the cross*, having slain the enmity thereby: And came and preached peace to you which were afar off, and to them that were nigh.
>
> EPHESIANS 2:13–17, EMPHASIS ADDED

The Day of the Lord is also the fulfillment of the *seventh day* of God's redemptive week, the millennial sabbath of rest: "there remains a rest [Gr. *sabbatismos*, literally "the keeping of a sabbath," *found nowhere else in the New Testament*] for the people of God" (Heb. 4:9). He that believes has already entered into rest. But here, he is also talking about not only God's *rest in creation*, and *His rest in redemption as well as the rest in Christ*, but there is also a sabbath rest for this earth. This is the millennial rest day, the seventh day of God's redemptive week. This day is designated as:

1. A keeping of sabbath rest (Heb. 4:9) which antedates the sabbath rest for Israel, which was a ceremonial not a moral law.

2. The Day of the Lord (2 Pet. 3:10)
3. The Day of God (2 Pet. 3:12)
4. The Day of the Lord as 1,000 years (2 Pet. 3:8)
5. The Day of Judgment and perdition of the ungodly (2 Pet. 3:7)
6. The last day (John 6:39–40, 44, 54; 11:24; 12:48). The day of the first resurrection is the start of the seventh or last day of God's redemptive plan.

To distinguish between "the last days" (Acts 2:17) and the "last day" (John 11:24), we have the following explanation. Since "one day is with the Lord as a thousand years, and a thousand years as one day" (2 Pet. 3:8), then *"the last days" began with Christ's first coming and will close with His second coming.* "The last day" brings us to the seventh day of God's week of redemption, to Christ's second coming and the first resurrection at the beginning of the millennial day. The Christian millennial day is that final Day of the Lord in His dealings as pertaining to earth. At the close of this sabbath day of rest, we look for the creation of a new heavens and the new earth "wherein dwells righteousness" (2 Pet. 3:13).

> And said unto me, *What seest thou*? And I said, I have looked, and behold *a candlestick all of gold*, with a bowl upon the top of it, and his seven lamps thereon, and seven pipes to the seven lamps, which are upon the top thereof.
>
> —Zechariah 4:2, emphasis added

> The mystery of the *seven stars which thou sawest* in my right hand, and the *seven golden candlesticks*. The *seven stars are the angels of the seven churches*: and *the seven candlesticks which thou sawest are the seven churches.*
>
> —Revelation 1:20, emphasis added

> And all these, though commended through their faith, did not receive what was promised, since God had provided something better for us, t*hat apart from us they should not be made perfect* [Gr. *teleioo*, bring to a close or fulfillment by event].
>
> —Hebrews 11:39–40, esv, emphasis added

> Then said the Lord unto me, Thou hast well seen: for I will hasten my word to perform it.
>
> —Jeremiah 1:12

> And the Lord answered me, and said, *Write the vision*, and *make it plain upon tables*, that he may run that readeth it. For *the vision* is yet for an appointed time, but at the end it shall speak, and not lie: though it tarry, wait for it; because it will surely come, it will not tarry.
>
> —Habakkuk 2:2–3, emphasis added

> Cast not away therefore your confidence, which hath great recompence of reward. For ye have need of patience, that, after ye have done the will of God, ye might receive the promise. For yet a little while, and *he that shall come will come, and will not tarry.* Now the just shall live by faith: but if any man draw back, my soul shall have no pleasure in him. But we are not of them who draw back unto perdition; but of them that believe to the saving of the soul.
>
> —Hebrews 10:35–39, emphasis added

The voice of him that crieth in the wilderness, *Prepare ye the way of the* Lord, *make straight in the desert a highway for our God.*

—Isaiah 40:3, emphasis added

Satan to be Released from the Bottomless Pit for a Season

At the conclusion of the millennial age, Satan is released for a season at the second resurrection of the wicked (unjust) dead and once again brings deception to the wicked just as he did to Eve in the beginning. All over the world Satan makes a last-ditch effort with those of the second resurrection of the wicked to come against the saints, but God devours them with fire out of heaven. The dead, both small and great, will stand before God at the great white throne and they will be judged according to their works which were written in the books; and, those not found written in the book of life will be cast into the lake of fire.

And *when the thousand years are expired, Satan shall be loosed out of his prison,* And shall go out to deceive the nations which are in the four quarters of the earth, Gog and Magog, to gather them together to battle: the number of whom is as the sand of the sea. And they went up on the breadth of the earth, and compassed the camp of the saints about, and the beloved city: and fire came down from God out of heaven, and devoured them. *And the devil that deceived them was cast into the lake of fire and brimstone, where the beast and the false prophet are, and shall be tormented day and night for ever and ever.* And I saw a great white throne, and him that sat on it, from whose face the earth and the heaven fled away; and there was found no place for them. And I saw the dead, small and great, stand before God; and the books were opened: and another book was opened, which is the book of life: and *the dead were judged out of those things which were written in the books, according to their works.* And the sea gave up the dead which were in it; and death and hell delivered up the dead which were in them: and *they were judged every man according to their works. And death and hell were cast into the lake of fire. This is the second death. And whosoever was not found written in the book of life was cast into the lake of fire.*

—Revelation 20:7–15, emphasis added

Promise to the Overcomer—Inherit All Things

And I saw a new heaven and a new earth: for the first heaven and the first earth were passed away; and there was no more sea. And I John saw the holy city, new Jerusalem, coming down from God out of heaven, prepared as a bride adorned for her husband. And I heard a great voice out of heaven saying, *Behold, the tabernacle of God is with men, and he will dwell with them, and they shall be his people, and God himself shall be with them, and be their God.* And God shall wipe away all tears from their eyes; and there shall be no more death, neither sorrow, nor crying, neither shall there be any more pain: for the former things are passed away. And he that sat upon the throne said, Behold, I make all things new. And he said unto me, Write: for these words are true and faithful. And he said unto me, It is done. I am Alpha and Omega, the beginning and the end. *I will give unto him that is athirst of the fountain of the water of life freely. He that overcometh shall inherit all things; and I will be his God, and he shall be my son.*

—Revelation 21:1–7, emphasis added

Epilogue
THE RIVER OF GOD

There is a river, the streams whereof shall make glad the city of God, the holy place of the tabernacles of the most High. God is in the midst of her; she shall not be moved: God shall help her, and that right early.
—Psalms 46:4–5

Introduction

We are on the verge of another significant move of God. Not just a revival or renewal but *a new thing on a grander scale*. Major events are coming.

> For the earth shall be filled with the knowledge of the glory of the Lord, as the waters cover the sea.
>
> —Habakkuk 2:14

Years ago my pastor admonished me with a quote from C.T. Studd's poem of the same name: "Only one life, 'twill soon be past, only what's done for Christ will last."[1] We should have a sense of urgency concerning our destiny. What is my purpose? Where is my place in the church of the Lord Jesus Christ? How can I fulfill God's intention for my life today without any regard for my past or present circumstances?

We know some things about the *river of God*, but I have never heard a message on the river of God. To see that vision of God's purposes you need to draw from the river of God. Ezekiel was among the captives in Babylon by the river of Chebar, where the heavens were opened, and *he saw visions of God*. It was there that the hand of the Lord was upon him, and he saw the appearance of the likeness of the glory of the Lord.

First the Natural, then the Spiritual

Between Hagerman and Twin Falls, Idaho, on Highway 30 you can see a once in a lifetime sight. Gushing from the steep canyon walls and cascading into the Snake River below are hundreds of natural springs. It is as if an underground river suddenly explodes from the earth itself. The Snake River Plains Aquifer, one of the world's largest ground water systems beneath Idaho's porous volcanic rock, water creeps through an area of several thousand square miles. The aquifer is like *an immense sponge*. The *porous basalt* holds vast amounts of water. It contains as much water as Lake Erie. The aquifer is recharged by *snow melt* and *rainfall* on the mountains to the north and east. The Big Lost River vanishes near Arco, where my wife, Ruth, and I pioneered a church in 1973, and the waters from that river reappear after traveling underground for 150 years. It provides drinking water for much of Southern Idaho. They tap the springs for irrigation and hydroelectric power and people make a living spawning trout and salmon in its waters. Some of the runoff is used for farmlands, feedlots, and cold-water fisheries. The springs and creeks provide critical habitat for plants and animals that need pristine water to survive. *A thousand cubic feet* per second of clean water flows into the Snake River.[2] The water is cold and crystal clear. Spiritually we need the waters from God's pristine waters to flow into our lives.

> Will a man leave the snow of Lebanon which cometh from the rock of the field? or shall the cold flowing waters that come from *another* [SC 2114, strange] place be *forsaken* [SC 5800, to loosen, relinquish, forsake or leave]?
>
> —Jeremiah 18:14, emphasis added

Both of these "forsaken" words appear in Jeremiah: 2:13; *forsake*, and 18:14; *leave*.

> Because my people hath forgotten me, they have burned incense to vanity, and they have caused them to stumble in their ways from the ancient paths, to walk in paths, in a way not cast up; To make their land desolate, and a perpetual hissing; every one that passeth thereby shall be astonished, and wag his head. I will scatter them as with an east wind before the enemy; I will shew them the back, and not the face, in the day of their calamity.
>
> —Jeremiah 18:15–17

In the late 1990s many from our church drove five hours to Brownsville Assembly in Pensacola, Florida, to drink from the cold flowing waters of revival there. We brought back revival to our church in Brooksville, Florida, and were revived and refreshed as revival was expanded.

Because of these things Jeremiah says in 23:9: "Mine heart within me is broken because of the prophets; *all my bones shake*; I am *like a drunken man*, and like *a man whom wine hath overcome*, because the Lord, and *because of the words of his holiness*." The word of the Lord came unto Jeremiah in chapter 2:13: "For my people have committed two evils; *they have forsaken me the fountain of living waters*, and hewn them out cisterns, broken cisterns, that can hold no water" (emphasis added).

Four principles of spiritual rivers

We need to notice four things—first the natural, then the spiritual:

1. Natural and spiritual rain produce natural and spiritual rivers, which is the Holy Spirit of God flowing.
2. The Lord is the fountain of living waters. To forsake or leave the waters is to forsake and leave Him!
3. To miss God and His provisions of refreshing and means of fruitfulness will bring judgment and barrenness to our soul. His refreshing is key to our survival!
4. We should not reject the truths which He deposits in *another* (strange) place for reasons like, "It is not coming to me the way that I imagined."

> Why, seeing *times* [Heb. *eth*] are not hidden from the Almighty, do they that know him not see his *days* [Heb. *yowm*]?
>
> —JOB 24:1, EMPHASIS ADDED

We have received some *spiritual rains* throughout the past 100 years, and yet I believe that the latter rains are not yet in their strength. We have seen many truths open up in the Word of God as never before. Those that hunger and thirst after God's Word and His righteousness are increasing. He said, "My doctrine shall drop as the rain" (Deut. 32:2). If we are to minister the Word of God, we must absorb His waters in us like a great underground lake. Our hearts need to be porous and open for the rain that God sends to our lives so that we will let the river of God flow forth.

Many hearts are in dry places. God wants to pour out of His Spirit upon His people. Without the rain, rivers dry up.

> Behold, God is great, and we know him not, neither can the number of his years be searched out. For he maketh small the drops of water: they pour down rain according to the vapour thereof: Which the clouds do drop and distil upon man abundantly. Also can any understand the spreadings of the clouds, or the noise of his tabernacle? Behold, he spreadeth his light upon it, and covereth the bottom of the sea.
>
> —JOB 36:26–30

> Who hath divided a watercourse for the overflowing of waters, or a way for the lightning of thunder; To cause it to rain on the earth, where no man is; on the wilderness, wherein there is no man; To satisfy the desolate and waste ground; and to cause the bud of the tender herb to spring forth? Hath the rain a father? or who hath begotten the drops of dew? Out of whose womb came the ice? and the hoary frost of heaven, who hath gendered it? The waters are hid as with a stone, and the face of the deep is frozen.
>
> —JOB 38:25–30

And the sweet psalmist of Israel, David, said:

> Thou visitest the earth, and waterest it: thou greatly enrichest it with *the river of God*, which is full of water: thou preparest them corn, when thou hast so provided for it. Thou waterest the ridges thereof abundantly: thou settlest the furrows thereof: thou makest it soft with showers: thou blessest the springing thereof. Thou crownest the year with thy goodness; and thy paths drop fatness. They drop upon the pastures of the wilderness: and the little hills rejoice on every side. The pastures are clothed with flocks; the valleys also are covered over with corn; they shout for joy, they also sing.
>
> —PSALMS 65:9–13, EMPHASIS ADDED

> Give ear, O ye heavens, and I will speak; and hear, O earth, the words of my mouth. *My doctrine shall drop as the rain, my speech shall distil as the dew, as the small rain upon the tender herb, and as the showers upon the grass.*
>
> —DEUTERONOMY 32:1–2, EMPHASIS ADDED

Zechariah urges us to ask for the rain *in the time of the latter rain*:

> Ask ye of the LORD rain in the time of the latter rain; so the LORD shall make bright clouds, and give them showers of rain, to every one grass in the field.
>
> —ZECHARIAH 10:1, EMPHASIS ADDED

The Lord comes to us as rain

> Come, and let us return unto the LORD: for he hath torn, and he will heal us; he hath smitten, and he will bind us up. After two days will he revive us: in the third day he will raise us up, and we shall live in his sight. Then shall we know, if we follow on to know the LORD: his going forth is prepared as the morning; and *he shall come unto us as the rain, as the latter and former rain unto the earth.*
>
> —HOSEA 6:1–3, EMPHASIS ADDED

Rivers in a dry place

> And *a man shall be as an hiding place from the wind, and a covert from the tempest; as rivers of water in a dry place,* as the shadow of a great rock in a weary land.
>
> —ISAIAH 32:2, EMPHASIS ADDED

> But there the *glorious* LORD *will be unto us a place of broad rivers and streams.*
>
> —ISAIAH 33:21, EMPHASIS ADDED

> And from thence they went to Beer: that is *the well* whereof the LORD spake unto Moses, *Gather the people together, and I will give them water. Then Israel sang this song, Spring up, O well; sing ye unto it.*
>
> —NUMBERS 21:16–17, EMPHASIS ADDED

It won't be the way you think

> Remember ye not the former things, neither consider the things of old. *Behold, I will do a new thing; now it shall spring forth; shall ye not know it? I will even make a way in the wilderness, and rivers in the desert.* The beast of the field shall honour me, the dragons and the owls: *because I give waters in the wilderness, and rivers in the desert, to give drink to my people, my chosen.* This people have I formed for myself; they shall shew forth my praise.
>
> —ISAIAH 43:18–21, EMPHASIS ADDED

> And there shall be upon *every high mountain,* and upon *every high hill, rivers and streams of waters in the day of the great slaughter, when the towers fall.* Moreover the light of the moon shall be as the light of the sun, and the light of the sun shall be sevenfold, as the light of seven days, *in the day that the* LORD *bindeth up the breach of his people, and healeth the stroke of their wound.*
>
> —ISAIAH 30:25–26, EMPHASIS ADDED

The reason for dry places

Don't be critical of various ways individuals manifest the glory of God. David's wife did, and she became barren (2 Sam. 6:16, 23). Avoid prejudging. God is sovereign and bears witness both with signs and wonders and with various kinds of miracles and gifts of the Holy Ghost according to His own will. "How shall we escape, if we neglect so great salvation" (Heb. 2:3)!

If you want no part of the river of God the Scripture says, "That saith to the deep, Be dry, and I will dry up thy rivers" (Isa. 44:27)! They wanted to be dry, so God sent no rain and He dried up their rivers! Pharaoh hardened his own heart first, and then God hardened Pharaoh's heart (Exod. 8:32; 9:12)!

Weeping and Supplications

Jeremiah prophesied the restoration and wide range (or general) return of God's people from the Assyrian captivity and Babylonian captivity, and he said:

> Behold, I will bring them from the north *country* [Heb. *erets*, or earth]...They shall come with weeping, and with supplications will I lead them: *I will cause them to walk by the rivers of waters in a straight way, wherein they shall not stumble.*
>
> —Jeremiah 31:8– 9, emphasis added

They had cried unto the Lord, "Arise ye, and let us go up to Zion unto the Lord our God" (v. 6). When we begin to cry out and weep and make supplication to the Lord, it is then that God will cause us to walk by the rivers of water. The proud need not apply. "God resists the proud, But gives grace unto the humble" (James 4:6, nkjv). You can generally perceive the hunger in a person when you lay hands on them. As Mary said, "He hath filled the hungry with good things; and the rich he hath sent empty away" (Luke 1:53). David said, "Deep calleth unto deep at the noise of thy water-spouts" (Ps. 42:7)—the deep of your heart calling out to the deep of God's heart! The rivers will begin to flow forth. They that worship God must worship in Spirit and in Truth (John 4:24)—from the heart as well as the head!

The approach to the river

> Before destruction the heart of man is haughty, and *before honour is humility.*
>
> —Proverbs 18:12, emphasis added

Weeping and tears go before joy, laughter, singing, and rejoicing!

> Therefore they shall come and sing in the height of Zion, and shall flow together to the goodness of the Lord, for wheat, and for wine, and for oil, and for the young of the flock and of the herd: and their soul shall be as a watered garden; and *they shall not sorrow any more at all.*
>
> —Jeremiah 31:12, emphasis added

> Then shall the virgin rejoice in the dance, both young men and old together: *for I will turn their mourning into joy,* and will comfort them, and *make them rejoice from their sorrow.* And I will satiate the soul of the priests with fatness, and my people shall be satisfied with my goodness, saith the Lord.
>
> —Jeremiah 31:13–14, emphasis added

> For I have *satiated* the weary soul, and I have *replenished every sorrowful soul.*
>
> —Jeremiah 31:25, emphasis added

The word *satiate* is Hebrew *ravah,* to slake the thirst, to quench the thirst, to make drunk, abundantly satisfy, to soak, to water abundantly.

Have you ever swum in a natural river for several hours? We went tubing down the Florida's

Ichetucknee River for about five hours; when you get out your fingers are all wrinkled and your skin is kind of water-logged. It is wonderful in the natural when you float down the river with trees on either side providing shade and the water is so crystal clear you can see the bottom ten to twelve feet below. But there that does not compare to after a time of soaking in the river of God. The feeling of saturation and satisfaction that you have spent time with your Creator, Redeemer, and Lover of your soul is just wonderful.

Natural and Spiritual House

The river of God comes from the house of the Lord. Ezekiel prophesies:

> Afterward he brought me again unto the door of the house; and, behold, *waters issued out from under the threshold of the house* eastward: for the forefront of the house stood toward the east, and the waters came down from under from the right side of the house, at the south side of the altar. Then brought he me out of the way of the gate northward, and led me about the way without unto the utter gate by the way that looketh eastward; and, behold, there ran out waters on the right side. And when the man that had the line in his hand went forth eastward, he measured *a thousand cubits*, and he brought me through the waters; the waters were *to the ankles*. Again he measured *a thousand*, and brought me through the waters; the waters were *to the knees*. Again he measured *a thousand*, and brought me through; the waters were *to the loins*. Afterward he measured *a thousand; and it was a river that I could not pass over: for the waters were risen, waters to swim in, a river that could not be passed over*. And he said unto me, Son of man, hast thou seen this? Then he brought me, and caused me to return to the brink of the river. Now when I had returned, behold, at the bank of the river were very many trees on the one side and on the other.
>
> —Ezekiel 47:1–7, emphasis added

The river of God issues out from *the doorway or entrance* of the house of God. That's where a thirsty soul finds God's river within God's house. Seeking the Lord where His people gather is vitally important for believers today.

> Not forsaking the assembling of ourselves together, as the manner of some is; but exhorting one another: and *so much the more, as ye see the day approaching*.
>
> —Hebrews 10:25, emphasis added

Too many today are missing the benefits of God's river because they totally abandon the house of God. It is most important to be faithful to God's purposes: "...and *unto him* shall the gathering of the people be" (Gen. 49:10c, emphasis added).

From whence came the river? From *the house of God*; from *the temple of God*. And what does the New Testament reveal about the house and the temple? Hebrews says:

> But Christ as a son over his own house; *whose house are we, if we hold fast the confidence and the rejoicing of the hope firm unto the end*.
>
> —Hebrews 3:6, emphasis added

> Now therefore ye are no more strangers and foreigners, but fellowcitizens with the saints, and of the household of God; And are built upon the foundation of the apostles and prophets, Jesus Christ himself

> being the chief corner stone; *In whom all the building fitly framed together groweth unto an holy temple in the Lord*: In whom ye also are builded together for an habitation of God through the Spirit.
>
> —Ephesians 2:19–22, emphasis added

> In the last day, that great day of the feast, Jesus stood and cried, saying, If any man thirst, let him come unto me, and drink. *He that believes on me, as the Scripture hath said, out of his belly shall flow rivers of living water.* (*But this spake he of the Spirit*, which they that believe on him should receive: for the Holy Ghost was not yet given; because that Jesus was not yet glorified.)
>
> —John 7:37–39, emphasis added

Modern Misconceptions

Jesus told Israel, who had rejected Him, "Behold, your house is left unto you desolate" (Matt. 23:38). Jesus had cast out all the money changers from the temple of God: "It is written, My house shall be called the house of prayer; but ye have made it a den of thieves" (Matt. 21:13). Jesus said in John 2:17 that "the zeal of thine house has eaten me up." He then said, "Destroy this temple, and in three days I will raise it up" (v. 19). They thought He was talking about the temple which took forty-six years to build, and they questioned how He could rear it up in three days. But He spoke of the temple of His body.

People are still missing the point today. The temple that God is building today is the household of God *not* a physical building. Paul says in Ephesians 2:20–22 that we "are built upon the foundation of the apostles and prophets, Jesus Christ himself being the chief corner stone; In whom all the building fitly framed together groweth unto *an holy temple*_in the Lord; In whom ye also are builded together for *an habitation of God through the Spirit*" (emphasis added). That is the well-spring of the river of God.

Paul said in Acts 17:24–28:

> God that made the world and all things therein, seeing that he is Lord of heaven and earth, *dwelleth not in temples made with hands*; neither is worshipped with men's hands, as though he needed any thing, seeing he giveth to all life, and breath, and all things; and hath made of one blood all nations of men for to dwell on all the face of the earth, and hath determined *the times* before appointed, and the bounds of their habitation; that they should seek the Lord, if haply they might feel after him and find him, though he be not far from every one of us: For in him we live, and move, and have our being.
>
> —Acts 17:24–28, emphasis added

God is not interested so much in what we *have* (our material possessions) but He is interested in our heart! If He has our heart, He has everything else!

> And it shall come to pass, that every thing that liveth, which moveth, whithersoever the rivers shall come, shall live: and there shall be a very great multitude of fish, because these waters shall come thither: for they shall be healed; and every thing shall live whither the river cometh. And it shall come to pass, that the fishers shall stand upon it from Engedi even unto Eneglaim; they shall be a place to spread forth nets; their fish shall be according to their kinds, as the fish of the great sea, exceeding many. But the miry places thereof and the marishes [pools or marshes] thereof shall not be healed; they shall be given to salt. And by the river upon the bank thereof, on this side and on that side, shall

> grow all trees for meat, whose leaf shall not fade, neither shall the fruit thereof be consumed: it shall bring forth new fruit according to his months, because their waters they issued out of the sanctuary: and the fruit thereof shall be for meat, and the leaf thereof for medicine.
>
> —Ezekiel 47:9–12

What is seen here is a picture of life-giving waters conducive for growth, not death but much fruitfulness and provision of healing. The same picture is seen in heaven:

> And he shewed me *a pure river of water of life, clear as crystal, proceeding out of the throne of God and of the Lamb.* In the midst of the street of it, and on either side of the river, was there the tree of life, which bare twelve manner of fruits, and yielded her fruit every month: and the leaves of the tree were for the healing of the nations.
>
> —Revelation 22:1–2, emphasis added

We also see here terms describing Eden, the garden of God, where the tree of life was placed in the midst of the garden, "and a river went out of Eden to water the garden" (Gen. 2:10).

The temple of God is your body, the local church and the universal church. We are God's husbandry (1 Cor. 3:9); God's garden (Song of Sol. 4:12); and the temple of God (1 Cor. 3:17); "whose house are we" (Heb. 3:6). That was the emphasis of the early church and that should be for the last days' church.

In a sermon preached by Dick Iverson in the early 1980s, he said, "Any doctrine that belittles the value of the local church in the life of a believer is not of God and is satanic in its origin."

God's Husbandry—God's Garden

Each one of us has a garden in our heart! "A garden enclosed is my sister, my spouse; a spring shut up, a fountain sealed . . . a fountain of gardens, a well of living waters" (Song of Sol. 4:12, 15).

The garden was locked. The Lord could not enter the garden to eat His pleasant fruits. Not only was the Lord of the garden not able to get into the garden, but once He gained entrance, He couldn't drink because the fountain was shut up and sealed. Many hearts are shut up and sealed to the Lord of the garden. The waters cannot flow out to bring life. Without the water of life, "joy is withered away from the sons of men" (Joel 1:12).

We cannot be blessed and we cannot be a blessing unless we give Him permission to come in and speak to us. The Lord cannot take pleasure in us, as He desires so much. "I am my beloved's, and *his desire is toward me*" (Song of Sol. 7:10).

> For thou shalt worship no other god: for the Lord, *whose name is Jealous, is a jealous God.*
>
> —Exodus 34:14, emphasis added

> For I am jealous over you with godly jealousy: for I have espoused you to one husband, that I may present you as a chaste virgin to Christ. But I fear, lest by any means, as the serpent beguiled Eve through his subtilty, so your minds should be corrupted from the simplicity that is in Christ.
>
> —2 Corinthians 11:2–3

Don't you want Him to come into your garden? Allow His Holy Spirit to bring a gusher of rivers of living water from your innermost being? He is the fountain of living waters! It is the waters of life that causes you to grow in the grace and knowledge of our Lord Jesus Christ. In the natural, a plant without water soon dies.

A well of water supplies the need of a few people. (See John 4:14.) The river of God provides life for many people! (See John 7:38–39.) Your life and ministry will yield fruit abundantly.

Just allow the river of God to flow over you, to quench your thirst for God; open up your heart and rejoice before Him! When your car breaks down, you will open the hood of that car and give permission to the mechanic (who you may not even know) to work on the engine! How much more should you open your heart to the Lord, your Creator and Redeemer, to do His good pleasure!

God wants our innermost being to be a channel for the river of God. For the river to stay in the channel, we must be right before God; otherwise we hinder the river from accomplishing God's purposes. The great problem is that many "living waters" cease to be living after they flow through men. There must be banks or channels of the river for it to benefit many. Rivers without banks become injurious.

> And the spirits of the prophets are subject to the prophets. For God is not the author of confusion, but of peace, as in all churches of the saints.
>
> —1 Corinthians 14:32–33

We need the discipline of the Holy Spirit in our lives. Bad habits, bad tempers, and our life in general needs to be cleansed and refined; otherwise the river is of no use. God's Word comes with the Holy Spirit and the water must remain pure. "Doth a fountain send forth at the same place *sweet water* and *bitter*?" (James 3:11).

There are *two rivers today*, two streams, one of God and one of Satan. Purity and holiness are characteristic of the river of God, but pollution and ungodliness are characteristic of the satanic flood of filth in the world today!

Warning on friendships

Lithia Springs County Park is located about five and one-half miles southeast of Brandon, Florida. From Lithia Major's Spring the discharge fluctuates between seven and seventy cubic feet per second, which waters find their way into the Alafia River. The Alafia River's water is dirty, murky, and dark (even black) water. The water from Lithia Springs is crystal clear. Together the waters (one-half black and one-half clear) flow together, yet separately, down the Alafia River for quite a distance before they merge together—not into a clear flowing stream but a black, murky, and dark colored stream. Just as in the natural, so it is in the spiritual. When a righteous person makes close fellowship and friendship with an unbeliever "chumming around" with that person for a time, there becomes an exchange. The purity of the believer takes on the negative nature of the unbeliever. "Can two walk together, except they be agreed?" (Amos 3:3). God hates mixture. And so the Scripture admonishes us:

> *Be ye not unequally yoked* together with unbelievers: for *what fellowship hath righteousness with unrighteousness*? and what *communion* hath *light with darkness*? And what *concord* hath *Christ with Belial*? or what *part* hath *he that believeth with an infidel*? And what *agreement* hath the *temple of God with idols*? for *ye are the temple of the living God*; as God hath said, I will dwell in them, and walk in them; and I will be their God, and they shall be my people. Wherefore come out from among them, and be ye separate, saith the Lord, and touch not the unclean thing; and I will receive you. And will be a Father unto you, and ye shall be my sons and daughters, saith the Lord Almighty.
>
> —2 Corinthians 6:14–18, emphasis added

When we are in right relationship with God, we add to the effectiveness of God's Word and we come forth as living water bringing life where ever we go. If God can find a willing vessel, He will speak; otherwise He will not speak.

During the Flood the fountains of the great deep were broken up. I believe before the Second Coming of the Lord, the fountains of the great deep will flow from the house of the Lord, and cause the *earth to be "filled with the knowledge of the glory of the* Lord, *as the waters cover the sea*" (Hab. 2:14). I see a mighty revival in store for the church!

A call to surrender, a call to humility, a call to purity and sweetness, a call to supplication

"Ask ye of the Lord rain in the *time* [Heb. *eth*] of the latter rain; so the Lord shall make bright clouds, and give them showers of rain, to every one grass in the field" (Zech. 10:1).

In which of these are you living today?

- Two Streams—Pure or Polluted
- Two Mysteries—Godliness or Iniquity
- Two Spirits—Truth or Error
- Two Kingdoms—Light or Darkness
- Two Seeds—Wheat or Tares
- Two Houses—God's House or Satan's House

So what shall we do? "Occupy till I come" (Luke 19:13), "See then that ye walk circumspectly, not as fools, but as wise, redeeming the time, because the days are evil" (Eph. 5:15–16), and, "...keep thyself pure" (1 Tim. 5:22c).

> For ye have need of patience, that, after ye have done the will of God, ye might receive the promise. *For yet a little while, and he that shall come will come, and will not tarry.* Now the just shall live by faith: but *if any man draw back, my soul shall have no pleasure in him.* But we are not of them who draw back unto perdition; but of them that believe to the saving of the soul.
>
> —Hebrews 10:36–39, emphasis added

1. Be patient after doing the will of God.
2. Know that Jesus is coming back again soon.

3. Don't backslide.

4. Believe in God's promises.

5. The fields are ripe for harvest—become a laborer.

> And that, knowing the time, that *now it is high time* to awake out of sleep: for now is our salvation nearer than when we believed.
>
> —ROMANS 13:11, EMPHASIS ADDED

> Why, seeing times are not hidden from the Almighty, do they that know him not *see his days*?
>
> —JOB 24:1, EMPHASIS ADDED

The following chart was designed from my class notes at Portland Bible College about 1982. The chart superimposes several features occurring during the seven one thousand years (the Lord's week). Included is a description about the chart's prominent features.

WEEK OF CREATION AND WEEK OF REDEMPTION

"God who at sundry times and in divers manners spake **in time past**

unto the fathers by the prophets. . .Heb. 1:1 "hath in these last days spoken unto us by his Son. . ." Heb. 1:2

	FORMER DAYS – "IN TIME PAST" *Ages Past*			**"LAST DAYS"** *Present Church Age*		**Ages**	**Future**
GOOD		**GOOD**	**GOOD**	**GOOD**	**VERY GOOD**	**GOD RESTS**	
1,000 years	2,000 years	3,000 years	4,000 years	5,000 years	6,000 years	7,000 years	Eternity
Light/Darkness Divided Gen. 1:1-5	Firmament Waters Divided Gen. 1:6-8	Sea/Earth & Seed Gen. 1:9-13	Sun, Moon, Stars Gen. 1:14-19 Given for Signs, Seasons, Days and Years	Fouls/Fish Gen. 1:20-23	Beast/Man/Woman Gen. 1:24-31	Earth Rests Gen. 2:1,2 Rev. 20:1-6 Day of Rest Satan Bound Heb. 4:1-10	New Heaven New Earth
Adam	**Noah**	**Abraham/Moses**	**David**	**Lord Jesus Christ**	**The Church**	**Christians**	**Redeemed**
Tree of Life Rev. 2:7	**Second Death** Rev. 2:11	**Hidden Manna & White Stone** Rev. 2:17	**Power over Nations David & Solomon** Rev. 2:26-28	**White Raiment/ Name in Book of Life** Rev. 3:4,5	**A New Name** Rev. 3:12	**Sit with Him in His Throne** Rev. 3:21	**Inherit All Things** Rev. 21:7
Day 1	**Day 2**	**Day 3**	**Day 4**	**Day 5**	**Day 6**	**Day 7**	
Edenic/Adamic	**Noahic**	**Abrahamic/ Mosaic/ Palestinian**	**Davidic**	**New**			**Everlasting**

Basic Chart from Class Notes taken at Portland Bible College, circa 1982

About the Chart

1. "Time Past" are the Former Days of Ages Past. *The four prior 1,000 years* God spoke through the prophets to the fathers.
2. "Last Days" from Christ's 1st coming unto His 2nd Coming. *Ages Future* refers to the Millennium and Eternity.
3. Each Day of Creation God said "It was good" *except for Day 2. God spared not the old world* saving only Noah and his family in Day 2 of the Week of Redemption. After creating everything in Day 6, God said, "It was *very good*." On Day 6 of the Week of Redemption there is a restoring of power to the Church prior to the 2nd Coming of the Lord Jesus Christ.
4. Each period of time in the Week of Redemption was "as" 1,000 years.
5. Each day of the Week of Creation had special features that correspond to the Week of Redemption:
   - Day 1 *Light and Darkness* -- Compare with the *righteous generations* of Seth and the *wicked generations* of Cain.
   - Day 2 *Waters Divided* -- Compare with the Flood of the 2nd 1,000 years.
   - Day 3 *Sea and Earth Seed*-- Compare with Seed of the Abrahamic Covenant.
   - Day 4 *Sun, Moon and Stars*-- Compare with signs of the Davidic Covenant (Jeremiah 33:19-26; Psalm 89)
   - Day 5 *Fouls and fish created*--Compare with Jesus sending out his disciples as "fishers of men" beginning the Church Age. (See also Matthew 13:47-50) Fouls symbols: Clean and Unclean
   - Day 6 *Beast, Man and Woman created*-- Compare with restoring the Church unto the "perfect man."
   - Day 7 *God Rests, the Sabbath of Creation*, cease and desist from work -- Compare with the "Sabbatismos," the last Day of the Week of Redemption.
6. *Overcomer Promises in Revelation in consecutive order* -- Compare with the Seven Days of Creation plus the 8th Day (Eternity). (See Chart with Overcomer Promises from the Book of Revelation)
7. *Days of the Week of Creation and Week of Redemption.*
8. Nine *progressive* Covenants that God initiated with man during the Week of Redemption: Edenic; Adamic; Noahic; Abrahamic; Mosaic; Palestinian; Davidic; New (The *Everlasting Covenant* contains the *eternal elements* of the others.)

BIBLIOGRAPHY

Anstey, Martin. *The Romance of Bible Chronology.* New York: Marshall Brothers, 1913. (An exposition of the meaning and a demonstration of the truth of every chronological statement contained in the Hebrew text of the Old Testament.)

Conner, Kevin J. *The Christian Millennium.* Victoria, AU: K.J.C. Publications, 2000.

———. *Restoration Theology.* Victoria, AU: K.J.C. Publications, 1998.

———. *The Seventy Weeks Prophecy: An Exposition of Daniel 9.* Victoria, AU: Acacia Press, 1981.

Conner, Kevin, and Ken Malmin. *The Covenants.* Portland, OR: Bible Temple Publishing, 1983.

———. *Interpreting the Scriptures.* Portland, OR: Bible Press, 1976.

Iverson, Dick. *Biblical Continuity: An Answer to Replacement Theory.* Portland, OR: City Publishing, 2007.

Iverson, Dick, and Bill Scheidler. *Present Day Truths.* Portland, OR: Bible Temple Publishing, 1975.

Lindsay, Gordon. *God's Plan of the Ages as Revealed in the Wonders of Bible Chronology.* Dallas, TX: Christ for the Nations, 1971.

Mauro, Philip. *The Wonders of Bible Chronology.* Swengel, PA: Bible Truth Depot, 1961.

Nave, Orville, and Anna Nave. *Nave's Study Bible: King James Version.* Grand Rapids, MI: Baker Book House, 1978.

Offiler, W. H. *God and His Bible.* Seattle, WA: Bethel Temple, 1946.

Patterson, W. W. *Bible Treasures from the Book of Daniel & the Book of Revelation.* Federal Way, WA: W. W. Patterson, 1987.

Pusey, Edward. *Daniel, The Prophet: Nine Lectures, Delivered in the Divinity School of the University of Oxford.* 1889. Reprint, Minneapolis: Klock & Klock, 1978.

Strong, James. *Strong's Exhaustive Concordance.* New York, Abingdon Press, 1890.

NOTES

Preface

1. "Isaac Newton Quotes," *Goodreads Inc.*, http://www.goodreads.com/author/quotes/135106.Isaac_Newton (accessed August 15, 2014).
2. Sir Isaac Newton, *The Correspondence of Isaac Newton*, ed. H.W. Turnbull, vol. 1 (Cambridge, UK: Royal Society University Press, 1959), 416.
3. Sir Francis Bacon quote from "Of Studies" (1597–1625) found at http://quotes.dictionary.com/histories_make_men_wise_poets_witty_the_mathematics (accessed July 29, 2014).

Introduction

1. Roger Pease, *Merriam-Webster Medical Dictionary* (Springfield, MA: Merriam-Webster, Inc., 2002), s.v. "bilateral symmetry."
2. "Symmetry in Biology," *Wikipedia*, last modified July 28, 2014, http://en.wikipedia.org/wiki/Radial_symmetry (accessed July 30, 2014).
3. *Webster's New Twentieth Century Dictionary*, s.v. "chronology."
4. *The Merriam-Webster Dictionary*, s.v. "chronology."
5. Martin Anstey, *The Romance of Bible Chronology* (New York: Marshall Brothers, 1913), explanatory notes.
6. Mick Sanderson, "Inclusive Reckoning Definitions," 2004, *Writer's Events*, http://www.writersevents.com/Words_Starting_with_I/incautious_income_tax/inclusive_reckoning_definition.html (accessed August 6, 2014).
7. *The American Heritage Dictionary of the English Language*, 4th ed., s.v. "epoch."

Chapter 1
Avoiding Bible Chronology Pitfalls

1. Dick Iverson, *Biblical Continuity: An Answer to Replacement Theory* (Portland, OR: City Publishing, 2007).
2. George Müeller quote found at *Liberty to the Captives*, http://www.libertytothecaptives.net/darby_mueller.html (accessed July 30, 2014).
3. David B. Curtis, "What is the Preterist View?" Berean Bible Church, http://www.bereanbiblechurch.org/transcripts/eschatology/what_is_the_preterist_view.htm (accessed July 30, 2014).
4. Edward Pusey, *Daniel, The Prophet: Nine Lectures, Delivered in the Divinity School of the University of Oxford* (1889; repr., Minneapolis: Klock & Klock, 1978), 192.
5. Ibid., 227.
6. Jose Carillo, "Must We Go Back to the First Noun to Find the Antecedent?" *Jose Carillo's English Forum*, July 18, 2011, http://josecarilloforum.com/forum/index.php?topic=1328.0, (accessed July 30, 2014).
7. John Parsons, "Unit Six–Learning Hebrew Pronouns," *Hebrew for Christians*, http://www.hebrew4christians.com/Grammar/Unit_Six/unit_six.html (accessed July 31, 2014).
8. Frank Boyd, *The Book of the Prophet Isaiah* (Springfield, MO: Gospel Publishing House, 1950), 114.
9. Philip Mauro, *Wonders of Bible Chronology* (Swengel, PA: Bible Truth Depot, 1961).

Chapter 2
Major Chronological Links

1. Anstey, *The Romance of Bible Chronology*, 9.
2. Pusey.
3. Albert Barnes, "Notes on the Whole Bible," *Internet Sacred Text Archive*, http://sacred-texts.com/bib/cmt/barnes/index.htm (accessed July 31, 2014).
4. Carl Keil and Franz Delitzsch, *Bible Commentary on the Old Testament* (Grand Rapids, MI: Eerdmans, 1949).

Chapter 3
Creation of All Things

1. A.M. Hodgkin, *Christ in All the Scriptures* (1909; repr., Westwood, NJ: Barbour and Co., 1989), pt. II, chap.1, "Genesis." (The entire book can be found online at http://www.thebookwurm.com/amh_tc.htm.)
2. Michael V. Frazier, "The 'Waw' Conjunctions of Genesis 1—Textual Support Against Gap and Day-Age Theories," *The Glorious Church* (blog), September 22, 2009 (11:30 p.m.), http://gloriouschurch.ning.com/profiles/blogs/the-waw-conjunctions-of (accessed July 31, 2014).
3. Terry Mortenson, "*Asah-Bara*," used by permission from Answers in Genesis, T. Winkler, found at http://www.answersingenesis.org/articles/aid/v2/n1/did-god-create-or-make (accessed July 31, 2014).
4. Terry Mortenson, "Did God Create (*Bara*) or Make (*Asah*) in Genesis 1," Answers in Depth, *Answers in Genesis*, http://www.answersingenesis.org/articles/aid/v2/n1/did-god-create-or-make (accessed July 31, 2014)
5. "Almond Lifecycle," About Almonds, *California Almonds*, http://www.almonds.com/consumers/about-almonds/almond-lifecycle (accessed August 6, 2014).

Chapter 4
Seeing Day 1

1. Anstey, "Antediluvian Patriarchs," *The Romance of Bible Chronology*, 30. Used by permission.
2. Mauro, 3–4.

Chapter 5
Seeing Day 2

1. Martin Anstey, "The Noah-Shem Connection," *The Romance of Bible Chronology*, 34. Used by permission.
2. Anstey, *The Romance of Bible Chronology*, 35.
3. Ibid., 34–35
4. John Kennedy, "Diagram of the Flood Year," chart in Anstey, *The Romance of Bible Chronology*, 35. Used by permission
5. Anstey, *The Romance of Bible Chronology*
6. Martin Anstey, "Postdiluvian Patriarchs," *The Romance of Bible Chronology*. Used by permission.

Chapter 6
Seeing Day 3

1. Anstey, *The Romance of Bible Chronology*.
2. Kevin Conner and Ken Malmin, *The Covenants* (Portland, OR: Bible Temple Publishing, 1983), 1. Used by permission.
3. Martin Anstey, "The Call, Promise, and Covenant of Abraham to the Exodus," *The Romance of Bible Chronology*. Used by permission.
4. Martin Anstey, "The Joseph-Moses Connection," *The Romance of Bible Chronology*. Used by permission
5. Martin Anstey, "The Seven Years' War," *The Romance of Bible Chronology*. Used by permission
6. Martin Anstey, "Chronology of the Period of the Judges," *The Romance of Bible Chronology*. Used by permission
7. Martin Anstey, "Israel under the Judges," *The Romance of Bible Chronology*. Used by permission.

Chapter 7
Seeing Day 4

1. Martin Anstey, *Chronology of the Old Testament* (Grand Rapids, MI: Kregel, 1973), and Mauro.
2. Mauro.
3. Anstey, *The Romance of Bible Chronology*.
4. James Strong, *Strong's Exhaustive Concordance*. New York, Abingdon Press, 1890, s.v. "kairos.
5. Frank Damazio, *Seasons of Revival—Understanding the Appointed Times of Spiritual Refreshing* (Portland, OR: BT Publishing, 1996), 371
6. Carillo
7. Stephen Amy, *Total Eclipse: Christ Returns: A Commentary on the Revelation of Jesus Christ* (Bloomington, IN: Author House, 2004)

8. Ibid
9. Kevin Conner, *The Christian Millennium* (Blackburn Victoria, Australia: K.J.C. Publications, 2000), 52–53). Used by permission
10. Kevin Conner and Ken Malmin, *Interpreting the Scriptures* (Portland, OR: Bible Press, 1976). Used by permission.

Chapter 8
Seeing Days 5 and 6

1. Conner, *The Christian Millennium*, 68.
2. Ibid.
3. Dick Iverson and Bill Scheidler, *Present Day Truths* (Portland, OR: Bible Temple Publishing, 1975), 36.
4. Kevin Conner, *The Book of Daniel: An Exposition* (Victoria, AU: K.J.C. Publications, 2004), 287. Used by permission
5. Conner, *The Christian Millennium*, 112.

Chapter 9
Seeing Day 7

1. Moritz Drechsler quoted in Franz Delitzsch and James Martin, *Biblical Commentary on the Old Testament* (Grand Rapids, MI: Eerdmans, 1973).
2. Martin Luther quoted in Franz Delitzsch and James Martin, *Biblical Commentary on the Old Testament* (Grand Rapids, MI: Eerdmans, 1973).
3. Franz Delitzsch and James Martin, *Biblical Commentary on the Old Testament* (Grand Rapids, MI: Eerdmans, 1973).
4. Strong's, s.v. "*sabbatismos*."

Epilogue
The River of God

1. C.T. Studd, "Only One Life, Twill Soon Be Past, Only What's Done for Christ Will Last," *Only One Life* (Paul Hockley blog), http://hockleys.org/2009/05/quote-only-one-life-twill-soon-be-past-poem/ (accessed August 5, 2014).
2. "The Eastern Snake River Plain Aquifer," *State of Idaho Oversight Monitor* (May 2005), found at http://www.deq.idaho.gov/media/552772-newsletter_0505.pdf (accessed August 6, 2014).

ABOUT THE BOOK

THE GENERAL PURPOSE of this book, *Seeing His Days,* is to challenge Christians, whether in church leadership or not, to become as the *Bereans* who "were more noble than those in Thessalonica, *in that they received the word with all readiness of mind, and searched the scriptures daily, whether those things were so*" (Acts 17:11, emphasis added). A more specific purpose is to help the reader *see* how God has fashioned and preserved the epochs of time based on a more sure chronology of the Old Testament from the first man, Adam, to the *last Adam,* who is the Lord Jesus Christ, and to show the seven 1,000 years, days of redemption, in God's design of the ages. From about 4,000 years of the Old Testament, to about 2,000 years of the church age, continuing on to the 1,000 years of the millennium that make up seven 1,000-year days of redemption, the book will challenge Christians today to walk in the Light of the Lord Jesus Christ.

ABOUT THE AUTHOR

JIM KAY WAS born in Tucson, Arizona, and born again in Chandler, Arizona. A turning point in his spiritual life came at age twenty-four after being refilled with the Holy Spirit, which caused a hunger for God's Word and strong desire to be a witness for the Lord. After completing a business management degree at San Jose State College in 1967, he earned a Bible and pastoral theology degree from Bethany Bible College in Santa Cruz, California, in 1970. He pastored churches in Idaho and Oregon from 1973 to 1980. The Lord directed him to Bible Temple in Portland, Oregon, where he became a deacon and elder while attending Portland Bible College from 1980 to 1982 and then teaching General Epistles and Old Testament History at PBC in 1983. He was sent out in 1983 with a team of about fifty people to build a church in Brandon, Florida. He has been serving the Lord at Grace World Outreach Church since 1993 in the ministry of Bible teacher and has served as elder for the past seven years. He has been studying Bible chronology since 1965, but more concentrated and focused studies from 1998 until 2014.

CONTACT THE AUTHOR

Email the author at jimwkay@gmail.com.